Contents

Preface   v

Acknowledgements   ix

1 Whole-school Issues   1
  Equal Opportunity policy   1
  Special Educational Needs policy   2
  Medical issues   13
  Bereavement   16
  Timetable implications of integration   21
  Breaktime arrangements   23
  School trips   26

2 Educational Implications of Disabilities and Medical Conditions   29
  Spina bifida and Hydrocephalus   30
  Muscular dystrophy   33
  Cerebral palsy   35
  Epilepsy   37
  Asthma   40
  Cystic fibrosis   42
  Spinal curvatures   43
  Limb deficiencies   45
  Visual impairment   46

3 Individual Education Plans   51

4 Resource Implications   57
   Environment   57
   Staffing   61

5 Differentiation   69
   Alternative means of recording work   69
   The environment   73
   Tasks   74
   Equipment   77
   Specialist equipment   78

Examples of Lesson Plans for Science and
Physical Education   83

Appendices   89

Useful Addresses   97

References   99

Preface

> Disabilities are socially constructed – change the way people think about disability and you eliminate the problems of disabled people.
>
> (Oliver 1988)

Towards integration

International campaigns to include all disabled children in education, emphasising the commitment of the world's leaders, were highlighted at the Convention on the Rights of the Child (United Nations 1989). The 'Education for All' programme which arose from the convention, aims to include all children who are in any way excluded from the benefits of schooling. Article 33 states the rights of disabled children to enjoy a full and decent life and also states that opportunities should be designed so that the child achieves 'the fullest possible social integration'.

At the UNESCO (United Nations Educational, Scientific and Cultural Organisation) World Conference on Special Needs Education (1994), the Salamanca statement, agreed by 92 governments and 25 international organisations, called for inclusion of disabled children to be the norm and adopted a new 'Framework for action'.

The statement adds: 'Regular schools with this inclusive orientation are the most effective means of combating discriminatory attitudes, creating welcoming communities, building an inclusive society and achieving education for all.'

However, whilst international resolutions are useful for providing frameworks, Mitler (1995) suggests that real progress depends on action at national and local levels.

In May 1990, the Council of the European Communities and Education ministers agreed that 'full integration into mainstream education should be considered as a first option in all appropriate cases'. This view was endorsed by the DFEE (Department for Education and Employment) Code of Practice (DFEE 1994) which advises that the needs of most pupils will be met in the mainstream and that children with special educational needs including those with statements should be educated alongside their peers in mainstream schools.

The benefits of including pupils with disabilities include: preparation of pupils for life, elimination of discrimination and the positive effect on all pupils. Mitler (1995) suggests that the effectiveness of our education systems will be judged by the extent to which they are able to prepare students for the community in which they live, and by the confidence with which they confront difficulties and obstacles. Integration can teach pupils with disabilities the skills of self-advocacy. The best way of ensuring that children can cope in mainstream society is to educate them in a totally integrated school.

Integration allows all pupils to learn about disabilities and can challenge the way they think. Most forms of prejudice are learned and are based on lack of knowledge. Mason (1995) suggests that everything which has been learned from anti-racism campaigns needs to be applied to people with disabilities, including positive images, role models, truthful histories, changing of the use of language, self-advocacy and anti-discriminatory legislation. All of these factors can be successfully addressed in an integrated mainstream school curriculum. Reiser (1995) emphasises benefits of integration to all pupils: 'this will lead to adults developing who are able to accept and value difference.'

Just as disabled children can learn from their physically able peers, so can the able-bodied learn from their disabled peers. The benefits of integration are summed up by a parent of a severely disabled child in mainstream school: '. . . but also for the able-bodied child. Let them see there is no fear or real differences because another child is in a wheelchair. Let them learn to help with little things like door opening, book gathering. Let them form friendships and let the able-bodied child appreciate her or his own good health.' (Hill 1996)

The changes in ethos, teaching styles and pupil management, together with any additional resources which may be necessary for successful integration, benefit all pupils. Teachers who differentiate lessons for some individual pupils have the resources instantly available for other pupils who may have similar needs.

The first step towards integration is that the school makes the decision to change. Such a decision must be a collaborative one, including staff, pupils and parents. Reiser (1995) suggests that 'successful integration is far more to do with attitudes than money!'

The attitudes of the school will be reflected in its whole-school policies, including equal opportunities and special educational needs. Resources are necessary to support the additional needs of pupils however, and the school will need to consider how these will be allocated in terms of buildings, staffing and equipment.

The role of the Special Needs Co-ordinator will be crucial to successful integration. Information about the educational implications of disabilities will be shared with all staff, together with co-ordination of provision, including support staff and equipment. Staff recruitment and training must address issues related to pupils with special educational needs in general and with physical disabilities specifically. 'Successful integration is dependent on collaboration and the setting up of structures that allow for achievement for all.' (Reiser 1995)

Such a collaborative approach demands consideration of whole-school issues such as equal opportunities, special educational needs, medication, bereavement, timetable, breaktime, movement and environment.

Acknowledgements

The author wishes to express her gratitude to June Pollard, for typing the manuscript; Mike Phillips, Filsham Valley School, for the photographic work; and Eugene Brunet and Paul Boxall, Filsham Valley School, for lesson plans. Also to the staff, parents and pupils of the Centre facility (Filsham Valley School) for their total commitment to the ethos of integration.

Chapter 1

Whole-school Issues

Traditionally, disabled children have been thought of in medical terms. They have been labelled, treated and frequently separated from mainstream education. Reiser (1995) however, argues that a 'social model' of thinking recognises that disabled people are not disabled by their impairment but rather by the lack of opportunity to take part in the normal life of the community on an equal level with others, due to social, physical and attitudinal barriers. This suggests that the principles of making provision for pupils with physical disabilities should be embedded in the whole-school equal opportunities policy. Historically, such policies have included issues such as race and gender. If special needs are included, schools have the opportunity to examine current provision and create an environment that will enhance learning for *all* pupils.

The policy should contain statements about: access, stereotyping, prejudice and achievement.

Equal Opportunity policy

Access

The policy should describe the physical environment, together with facilities for disabled people. If access is difficult or not possible, the policy should address areas for development, including bids for building alterations, or small equipment such as ramps.

Statements about access should refer to equality of opportunity for learning, including the curriculum, resources and extracurricular activities and trips.

Stereotyping

The school should state its intent to value individual achievement and skills. Displays, assemblies, learning resources and libraries should reflect the diversity of society and should celebrate difference.

The curriculum should include positive images of disabled people. Careers advice should encourage disabled pupils to achieve beyond stereotyped roles and expectations.

The school's expectations of its pupils has a major role in overcoming stereotyping. If disabled pupils are expected to be included in all activities, then attitudes of the non-disabled are constantly challenged.

Prejudice

The equal opportunities policy needs to demonstrate the steps taken by the school to create an environment in which all pupils can thrive and succeed. This requires education about disability in the curriculum. A great deal of prejudice can be erased through informative education.

Guidelines will be required to formalise procedures for staff if prejudice occurs. Such guidelines may be similar to existing policy on racism, bullying or name-calling.

Achievement

Schools should celebrate achievement for all pupils, regardless of ability. Statements in the equal opportunities policy should reflect the equal value of all in the community and the need for all staff and children to respect each other, regardless of difference.

The Technical and Vocational Experience Initiative South East Race and Gender Network suggests that a whole-school policy should include:
- statement of entitlement
- aims and rationale
- policy statements on key issues
- action plans for implementation
- action plans for specific situations
- procedures for monitoring
- procedures for evaluation
- strategies for dissemination, consultation and review.

Such areas would seem to be equally suitable when considering the inclusion of physical disabled students in the equal opportunities policy.

Special Educational Needs policy

The governing body of the school, working closely with the headteacher and SENCO (Special Needs Co-ordinator) should determine the school's special educational needs policy, having regard to the DFEE Code of Practice. This policy should be closely linked to the school's equal opportunities policy.

The policy should include the following.

- Aim of the school.
- Objectives.
- The role of the SENCO, who should be named.
- Admission guidelines.
- The arrangements for co-ordinating provision for pupils with special educational needs, for example, the staffing deployment.
- The arrangements for allocating resources.
- Identification, assessment and provision for all pupils with special educational needs.
- Information relating to any special facility which improves access for pupils with special educational needs.
- Information about the school's staffing policies and partnerships with bodies beyond the schools.

In relation to pupils with physical disabilities, the SENCO should consider the following aspects when developing a special educational needs policy.

Aim

The aim of the special educational needs policy should reflect aspects of the whole-school aims and the equal opportunities policy.

Objectives

The policy should include a number of objectives, such as the following:
- To ensure early identification of any special educational needs.
- To ensure access to a broad, balanced and relevant curriculum.
- To make a flexible response to individual needs and make efficient use of resources.
- To work together with other organisations with the aim of making the best use of resources.
- To ensure that provision is regularly monitored and evaluated.

Role of the Special Needs Co-ordinator (SENCO)

The role of the SENCO is crucial to the successful integration of pupils with physical disabilities. He or she must be able to liaise with and advise other staff, consult with external agencies and manage the special educational provision within the school.

The Code of Practice has defined the role of the SENCO and has included many different functions. Given all of these considerations, it is vital that the SENCO is either a member of the senior management team or has regular access to it. Many schools now recognise the importance of the role and allocate the SENCO the appropriate status, both in terms of pay and position.

The Code of Practice states that the role includes the following:
- Day-to-day management of the school's special needs policy.
- Liaison with fellow teachers.
- Contribution to in-service training.
- Co-ordination of provision for pupils with special educational needs.
- Maintenance of the school's special educational needs register and oversight of records.
- Liaison with parents of pupils with special educational needs.
- Liaison with external agencies.

Day-to-day management of special educational needs policy

The SENCO's daily role includes deployment of resources, including staff, administration duties, liaison with staff and, usually, teaching.

For many pupils with physical disabilities there is a recognised level of support required, which may not change. However, for some children the needs change regularly. Some pupils with severe medical conditions may require a different level of support every day. The SENCO needs to adjust provision according to priority of need. Daily meetings with support staff may be extremely beneficial. A ten-minute meeting, held at the beginning of each day, could be used as a 'briefing' meeting to ensure that pupils have an adequate level of support.

The same briefing meeting could also be used to redeploy equipment if necessary. Support staff should be aware of the lesson content for that day and may be able to highlight areas of concern. For example, two pupils may require access to the same computer. Most pupils with physical disabilities have to share resources within the school and there may be clashes occasionally.

The administration duties of the SENCO are various and can be very time-consuming. They include writing review notes, collecting evidence, assessing needs, writing letters, making referrals, co-ordinating annual reviews and individual education plans, all administration regarding the placement of pupils on the special needs register, including termly reviews. Therefore, each day, SENCOs need to maintain the administration demands of their role. Some schools have now recognised the work load imposed on the SENCO and have either reduced teaching hours or have allocated secretarial support. There is little doubt that secretarial support is extremely beneficial, since it uses skilled staff who can complete the same paperwork in less time. Such staff could be allocated duties such as collection and distribution of paperwork for reviews and individual education plans, word-processing of communications and storage of information. This releases the SENCO to use the special educational needs teaching skills for which she or he was employed. A recent conference held by the DFEE, 'Code of Practice – two years on', concluded that many SENCOs indicated a need for greater clerical support.

Liaison with other staff

The SENCO manages support staff and in a larger school may also manage other special educational needs teachers. In addition, they are generally expected to advise and support all staff in their management of pupils with physical disabilities. This support may take the form of providing in-service training on various aspects of disability. It might also include teaching alongside colleagues, offering advice where appropriate.

Provision of in-service training

SENCOs are expected to contribute to the school staff development policy by providing in-service training for fellow staff. When considering pupils with physical disabilities, the training might include such topics as specific conditions and the educational implications, safe lifting techniques, first aid procedures and differentiation. SENCOs would not necessarily by expected to deliver the courses, but should investigate possible contracts for local education authority staff or local organisations that may be prepared to do so (see 'Training/staff development', page 67).

Maintenance of special educational needs register and record keeping

All pupils with special educational needs must be placed on the school's special educational needs register. Any changes to the stage at which a child is placed, made as a result of reviews, must also be recorded. For pupils with physical disabilities, it is unlikely that there will be a great deal of movement, as many children with severe disabilities have a statement of special educational needs. However, there is a number of pupils whose condition deteriorates.

The SENCO is responsible for all record keeping at every stage of special educational needs. This includes all paperwork for individual education plans and reviews, whether termly or annual (see Chapter 3 'Individual Education Plans').

Liaison with parents

Parents have a very important role in the successful integration of pupils with physical disabilities and SENCOs need to consider how to create effective communication with them. Schools should have a policy which states the minimum frequency of contact with parents, including parent consultations and reports. It is recognised that parents of pupils with special educational needs may require more consultation. Some parents of pupils who are seriously ill may even require daily contact.

The SENCO should consider how such consultations can be maintained. For example, key staff may be identified to act as a regular point of contact for parents. In primary schools, this is often the class teacher or support assistant. Secondary schools may identify one key person to a year group. Some schools have arranged special educational needs consultation evenings, inviting parents of pupils with special educational needs to meet informally and discuss relevant issues.

Not all contact needs to be 'face to face'. Liaison can take the form of a home–school diary or memos, sent home with the child. It may prove impractical to anticipate regular meetings in school with many individual parents.

Co-ordination of provision

Under the Code of Practice, provision for pupils with special educational needs is linked to five stages: stages 1 to 3 being school-based approaches and stages 4 and 5 being equivalent to the stage at which a pupil may be formally assessed for a statement.

There are difficulties in demonstrating a clearly-structured approach that can be linked to each stage of provision for pupils with physical disabilities, as the school response depends to some extent on the pupil's individual ability to cope with his or her condition. Some pupils cope in mainstream with very few additional resources, whilst some others may require full-time ancillary support. Also, as physical disabilities can be progressive and/or regressive, provision needs to be immediate and flexible. However, Tables 1.2–1.6 attempt to demonstrate what might be possible for a school when responding to different levels of need.

Table 1.1 suggests provision that could be made by the school for pupils with physical disabilities at Stages 1, 2 or 3. Table 1.2 suggests further provision that could be made if the pupil has been formally assessed for a statement. As many pupils have learning difficulties associated with their physical disabilities, Tables 1.3–1.6 suggest a five-staged approach to meeting those additional needs. Further details of provision are included in Chapter 5, 'Differentiation', which gives examples in subject areas.

Tables 1.1 to 1.6
A staged approach to meeting special educational needs in mainstream schools

Table 1.1 Physical disabilities: Stages 1–3.

Strategies	Examples
Differentiation	Classroom management (use of space, seating pupil near exit, near plug for laptop work; use of grids/tables to limit amount of writing). Differentiated tasks for P.E./practical tasks/ school trips, etc. Access to computers. I.E.P. Stages 2 to 4 only.
Pastoral support	Identification of key member of staff to give additional support – working with group tutor.
Adapted environment	Use of lifts, ramps, separate fire routes. Toilet facilities for disabled students. Rest area.
Adapted equipment	Technical aids (pencil grips, adapted P.E. equipment (e.g. bats/foam javelin/wristbands for unihoc), keyboard guards, tracker balls, non-slip mats. Vari-height tables/sinks, foot rests, sloped desks).
Curriculum support	In-class support by class/general assistant – for practical help (in Te/Sc/Art etc.) – for curriculum (used as amanuensis/reader).
Personal care support	Advice from physiotherapist/O.T./speech therapist.

Table 1.2   Physical disabilities: statemented.

Any combination of strategies employed at Stages 1–3 plus.

Strategies	Examples
Differentiation	As shown in Table 1.1 plus I.E.P. outlining individual programme based on statement of need.
Adapted environment/equipment	As shown in Table 1.1. May have personal aids provided by Health Authority (walking frame, wheelchair, splints, augmentative communication device).
Curriculum support	High percentage full-time ancillary support for lessons (amanuensis/communicator/reader etc.) Special arrangement for exams (use of amanuensis/additional time etc.)
Personal care support	Ancillary support to – administer medical treatment – help with toileting arrangements – implement physiotherapy programme – help with practical tasks (e.g. dressing) – help with meal times. Physiotherapy – advice and treatment in school. Speech therapy – advice and treatment in school. Occupational therapy – advice and treatment in school. G.P./School nurse – treatment and first aid.

Table 1.3 Learning difficulties: Stage 1.

Strategies for managing pupils with learning difficulties at any Stage
may be combined with strategies for managing physical disabilities.

Strategies	Examples
Differentiated tasks	Varied response to task in place of writing (cloze technique, cutting and pasting, use of grids/tables, pictorial/oral response, role-play). Simplified task – high quality/less quantity. 'Tiered' levels for test/exams.
Differentiated materials	Larger text, simplified language, additional illustrations. Homework printed for pupil or scribed by assistant.
Additional time	Extra time allowed for homework/tests.
Access to additional support	Encouragement to attend 'homework help' club, lunchtime and evenings. Staffed by assistants/teachers. Encouragement to attend spelling club – 1 session per week, lunchtimes – staffed by SEN teacher.
Monitoring by group tutor	Weekly review of homework diary and discussion – progress with parents at parents evening.

Table 1.4 Learning difficulties: Stage 2.

Any strategies employed at Stage 1 plus.

Strategies	Examples
Monitoring by SEN Co-ordinator/ SEN teacher	Weekly meeting with pupil to establish welfare and progress (informal). Liaison with tutor. Termly review of I.E.P.
I.E.P. written and implemented	All relevant subject teachers contribute where provision is over and above normal provision for group. Targets specified and strategies outlined. Parents consulted and given summary sheet.
Use of readers where appropriate	Can use ancillary assistants where available, or mixed groups to allow pupil support.
Parental support	Parents invited to contribute to termly review and offer help at home (e.g. reading practice on a regular basis).

Table 1.5 Learning difficulties: Stages 3 and 4.

Any combination of strategies employed at Stage 1 or 2 plus.

Strategies	Examples
Advice from L.S.S.	Contact L.S.S. teacher for advice (individual programmes/materials, etc.).
Differentiated tasks	May need to use differentiated levels of work in recognised schemes (Hu, for example, in addition to those employed in Stage 1).
Support from L.S.S.	Year 7 only – 1 session per week individual/small group tuition – withdrawn from mainstream lessons.
Attendance at curriculum support	Withdrawn for numeracy/literacy skills at Key Stage 3 for additional teaching.
Use of amanuensis	Work to be scribed following dictation.
Use of reader	Use of reader for end of module tests, exams, etc., other than in English.
Access to computer	Could use laptop or networked computer for word processing and spell checking facility.
Access to spellmaster	Availability of spellmaster in class for individual use.

Table 1.6 Learning difficulties: statemented.

Any combination of strategies employed at Stages 1 to 4 plus.

Strategies	Examples
I.E.P. written and implemented	Targets written which support needs which have been identified in statement.
Curriculum support	Full or part-time ancillary/teaching support to enable student to access curriculum with amanuensis. Small group teaching. As aid to differentiation, etc. Special arrangements for exams (longer time, use of amanuensis, reader, communicator). Provision of laptop for personal use. Provision of spellmaster for personal use.
Withdrawal from some areas of curriculum	May need to be considered if learning difficulties severe (e.g. second modern foreign language in Year 8).

Many pupils with physical disabilities have associated medical conditions and schools will need to take account of this when making special educational provision. Medical care should be included in the pupil's individual education plan and should follow the agreed school policy which should have statements on principles, staffing, training, processing information, role of medical staff and procedures.

Principles

It should be accepted that some pupils may require medical treatment or medication during school hours. There should, therefore, be a full and agreed school policy on first aid and medical treatment, which is drawn up in consultation with all staff and agreed with parents, which states as its main aim that pupils' health and safety within school is of paramount importance.

Staffing

If a school intends to make provision for a disabled pupil with a medical condition, careful consideration needs to be given to the question of who will administer treatment. As a general rule, staff cannot be instructed to give treatment or medication. In many schools, classroom assistants and/or school secretaries volunteer to do so. However, a 'volunteer' arrangement cannot be binding. As medical conditions become more severe or difficult to manage, including the need for injections, rectal valium, suctioning of tracheotomy tubes, etc., some schools are now employing a part-time or full-time qualified nurse. This gives school staff confidence that professional medical help is always available. It also gives reassurance to headteachers at a time when increasing numbers of legal actions against staff in cases of accidents are occurring. Other benefits of employing a qualified nurse are that aspects of PSE can be enhanced by support from a medical expert for all pupils. However, this should not detract from the fact that in many cases support staff are prepared to perform some medical duties in order that a pupil can be integrated.

Training

Training of staff is essential in a school where medical procedures are being followed. It is vital that the school gathers as much information as possible from all available sources, including physiotherapists, family doctor, consultant and parents. In many cases, parents know more about their child's condition than anyone else and are in a very good position to offer advice and support to school staff. Many

Medical issues

parents are willing to attend training sessions at school to help staff who will be working with their child.

Local authorities frequently offer training to support staff on a variety of medical conditions such as epilepsy, asthma and diabetes. Alternatively, specific conditions may require training from school nurses or consultant paediatricians. It is necessary for the SENCO to establish good relationships with professionals in the local health authorities, so that medical information about the pupil can be shared. In many authorities, health service professionals are invited to contribute to the annual review of pupils who have a statement of special educational needs and this practice could be extended to any pupil with a serious medical condition who requires reviews on progress.

Many areas now offer the 'First aid at work' qualification – a four-day course covering major aspects of first aid. Area health and safety policies contain regulations regarding numbers of staff requiring first aid qualifications.

Information

The school policy will need to consider how much medical information about a child is shared and how it can be circulated to staff on a 'need-to-know' basis. All medical details should be stored in a central area, but staff should know which children in their classes have conditions such as epilepsy, asthma and diabetes and be aware of symptoms which may indicate the need for medical help. In cases where, for example, a pupil has a life-threatening condition, the staff working with him or her need to know of symptoms and the emergency action that may be necessary.

One means of ensuring such communication is to issue a single-sheet information page to all relevant staff, listing symptoms to be aware of and immediate action. The sheet can be general, giving information about a common condition (see Appendix 1), or could be specific to a pupil (see Appendix 2).

Role of medical staff

This section of the policy should detail the role of the co-ordinator for medical treatment and the role of the duty medical staff, if different.

Co-ordinator for medical procedure

The school will require a named member of staff who will be responsible for monitoring the medical procedure in school, as set out in the policy. A suggested role will include:
- Monitoring the duty rota for first aid/medical treatment on a weekly basis;

- Monitoring the procedure for administration of medication/ treatment;
- Checking and maintaining the first aid boxes around the school;
- Liaising with staff in charge of school trips;
- Liaising with school health and safety officer;
- Arranging cover for medical duties in case of absence.

Duty medical staff (daily basis)

The school may appoint more than one person as being responsible for the medical policy on a daily basis. Their role might include:
- Administering all daily medication and treatment;
- Being available for personal care needs of pupils;
- Being on call for illness and accidents;
- Assisting in daily physiotherapy programme, if appropriate;
- Accompanying pupils to hospital if required;
- Liaising with parents in cases of medical illness or accident.

Medical procedure

Medical procedures in school should follow any available County guidelines. All procedures should be carefully documented. Medication brought into schools should be clearly labelled, with the name of the pupil, precise dosage and time of medication. With the exception of asthma inhalers, which should remain with the pupil, all medicines should be handed to the appointed member of staff. The school may need to consider the provision of a refrigerator for some types of medication. A lockable medical cabinet must also be available.

Medication given in school should be given by authorised staff only, with parental consent. Clear records should be kept of all medication given, together with the signature of the pupil and staff, outlining the dosage, time and date.

In the case of medical treatment, the timing and type of treatment should be recorded and a signature given. If possible, two members of staff should be present.

Medical logs should be in the form of a book, preferably not loose-leaf, with numbered pages.

In secondary schools, pupils should be encouraged, wherever appropriate, to perform their own treatments. Many pupils are capable of administering their own injections, blood tests, catheter changes, etc., under supervision and they should be persuaded to be as independent as possible. Staff will need to be aware of emotional development and dependency on others.

Procedures to be followed for unwell or injured pupils should follow general school policy. However, medical staff need to be aware that some symptoms experienced by an unwell disabled pupil may be indications of a more severe condition. For example, for a child who has hydrocephalus, a headache may be a symptom of a faulty shunt. In such cases, the parents should be informed immediately.

Bereavement

Integrating pupils with physical disabilities in mainstream schools highlights the need for teachers to prepare pupils for occasional death and bereavement. This is particularly true for schools which integrate children who are terminally ill or who have a life-threatening condition. Preparation by the staff will help pupils to cope with the loss. Ward (1995) suggests that 'if we don't mourn losses at the time they happen, major problems, for example, severe depression, can be triggered off when later losses occur.'

The school's ability to cope with death will be largely dependent on its preparation for it. Preparation for bereavement will include the development of guidelines for coping with bereavement and curriculum planning.

Curriculum planning

Loss and death education had no major part in the school curriculum until recently, but should now be an integral part of the Personal and Social Education programme, at each Key Stage. The subject is also included in all stages of Religious Education. Schools are expected to develop their own syllabus for class work.

Ideally, a small group of staff should work together in developing the curriculum content. Those staff should have come to terms with losses themselves, and should not have been recently bereaved. Short training courses which explore the feelings of loss and consider the issue of good listening skills, are usually available in local areas to education staff.

The curriculum for death and bereavement should include:
- *Understanding loss* – growing up, going to school, moving home, losing an object, birth of a sibling, death of a relative.
- *Understanding feelings* – for example, encouraging children to talk about, for example, happiness, excitement, anger, fright, sadness.
- *Understanding death* – ageing, the life cycle, seasons, funeral customs.

Projects can be undertaken which include creative writing, stories and poems, drama work, visits to cemeteries, etc.

Death of a pupil – the school's response

The school will need to consider its response to the death of a pupil, and may wish to develop either a policy or guidelines for staff. There are many practical requirements which work best when they are planned, although there should be a flexible approach depending on individual circumstances. In particular, family wishes should always be taken into account.

The effects of the policy will depend on wide consultation with all staff, parents and governors, and when developed and agreed will help staff to cope with the loss.

When a pupil dies, the school may wish to consider communication, and short-term and long-term responses to pupils.

Communication

It is helpful for a school to name a member of staff who will take responsibility for informing the community about the death of a pupil. Usually a senior member of staff will inform the governors, colleagues and pupils. It is also beneficial to the school if there is an agreed procedure for informing pupils. Information can be given in year groups or classes for example, and the school may need to judge who is the best person to tell the pupils. There is a wider group of relevant people who may also need to know, including external agency staff, professionals working in the health and social services department and advisory staff. In some instances, there may be a wish to give information to parents and the school may need to supply a short written message.

Short-term response

In addition to informing the school community about the death of a pupil, other issues need to be considered so that the school can make the best possible response. In the short-term, the school will need to make arrangements to support the family, staff and friends of the pupil.

Counselling
Action taken might include making arrangements for in-school counselling. Some schools have their own counsellor appointed to the staff. Others use organisations such as CRUSE, which has expertise in bereavement counselling for adults and children.

Support for the family
Cards and messages sent to the bereaved family are often appropriate at this time. The school may also wish to consider sending an appropriate member of staff to visit the parents.

Funeral arrangements
Schools have differing arrangements for funeral attendance, which may be linked to the age of the pupil. It will probably be appropriate for a member of the school staff to attend the funeral, with the family's consent. If other parents or pupils wish to attend, the family

should be consulted. It is essential that their views are sought first.

Staff may also wish to consider whether flowers or a wreath will be sent from the school, and who will pay. In some schools, governors pay for such items, whilst in others a small fund is available.

Long-term response

Counselling

For some pupils, a small number of sessions with a trained counsellor may be sufficient. For others, longer term counselling may be required. Schools should be guided by the counsellor but will need to make timetabled provision if regular intervention in school is required.

The SENCO should also be aware that if a pupil died as a result of his or her disability – muscular dystrophy, for example – other pupils with the same condition may require help to come to terms with their own mortality.

Memorial

Many schools offer pupils the opportunity to hold short ceremonies in memory of their friend. This may be particularly helpful if the funeral was not attended. Pupils can be encouraged to write or speak about the pupil. It may be appropriate to consider tree or shrub planting in memory, together with a plaque to celebrate the life of the child. Such responses can have a positive contribution in the management of bereavement. The type of memorial service may be arranged according to the age and needs of the pupils.

Having such guidelines on managing the death of a disabled pupil, prepared in consultation with all staff before such an event occurs, will serve to help staff at a time when emotional responses may be varied. Having administration and support mechanisms in place gives staff more time to support parents, pupils and colleagues at what is always a distressing time. It also provides staff with a carefully considered and sympathetic response, which is always appreciated by bereaved parents.

Death of a pupil – responding to bereaved pupils

Stages of grief

When a child in school dies, teachers need to be aware of the impact of the death on the pupils who have been bereaved, particularly those who were in the same class or tutor group. Bereaved children may go through some or all of the following stages of grief (Ward 1995):

- shock and disbelief
- denial

Awareness of feelings such as
- longing
- anger
- depression
- guilt
- anxiety
- acceptance.

Most people need to work through all the stages in order to come to terms with the loss, but individuals progress at different rates. Some children may get 'stuck' at a stage and may require specialist help to cope with the death.

The following section offers a brief description of each stage, together with some strategies for staff in making their response. Probably the most important response is to acknowledge how the bereaved pupil is feeling.

It should not be forgotten that other staff may also be grieving for the pupil and colleagues will need to recognise any difficulties being experienced at a time when teachers are trying to support the pupils in their care.

Shock and disbelief

Pupils who are told of a friend's death may go into a state of shock. They may react hysterically or may appear apathetic, withdrawn or unnaturally calm.

Strategies

Be aware of the effects of shock.

Be patient and nurturing.

Be prepared to listen.

Denial

Bereaved pupils may deny the death. They may behave as if the child was still alive and refuse to acknowledge the loss. This stage of grief can last for minutes, hours, days or for a very long period, even years.

Strategies

Encourage pupils to talk about their feelings.

Encourage pupils to write to the person or about the death.

Encourage pupils to read relevant, age appropriate, books.

Longing

Pupils may need to remember the loss over and over again. They may consider trying to establish a reason for the death and wish to talk about the actual circumstances of it. They may have vivid dreams of the dead child.

Strategies

Be prepared to give time to listen.

Allow child to express his or her feelings.

19

Anger

Pupils may express anger about the death. The anger may be transferred to the parents, the health services, God and sometimes, themselves. Such anger may be expressed at any time after the death.

Strategies

Reassure the pupil that it is all right to feel angry.

Allow the pupil to express his or her feelings.

Offer alternative means of expressing anger – shouting, stamping, drawing, bursting balloons, etc.

The school might offer 'anger management' courses during PSE lessons.

Depression

Depression is very common after bereavement and can be described as feelings of emptiness, pain and despair. Symptoms of depression can include crying, withdrawal and apathy.

Strategies

Allow the pupil to talk about his or her feelings. This may require extra pastoral support.

Allow the pupil to cry – give time out of class if necessary.

Offer the option of professional counselling if the pupil and his or her parents agree.

Guilt

Pupils often feel guilty about their response to the dead child when he or she was alive. They may wish they had given more attention, been more friendly or said something which was left unsaid. There is sometimes a tendency to idealise the dead person. Pupils may feel guilty about enjoying themselves during such a sad time.

Strategies

Acknowledge the child's feelings.

Try to explain that such feelings are normal.

Help the child to recognise the positive effects of their relationship, prior to the death.

Anxiety

Some pupils may become very anxious, even panicked, about the death. If there are several pupils with disabilities in the school, they may become anxious about their own condition.

Strategies

Reassure or talk to pupils with disabilities about their condition; this may need to be regularly reinforced.

Give time to talk to anxious pupils.

Refer to specialist counsellors if necessary, with parental consent.

Acceptance

Acceptance of a child's death may never occur, or may only occur during the second year after the death, when the anniversary of the death has been acknowledged. This allows the bereaved person to come to terms with the loss and recognise that nothing can be changed.

The age of the bereaved child

When teachers are considering their response to bereaved pupils following the death of one of the group, it is necessary to recognise that the age of the pupils can affect their response to death. Young children process information differently from adults. Typically, depending on emotional development, children react to death in the following ways.

1 to 3 years Very young children do not understand that death is permanent. They may constantly ask when the dead person is coming back. They may become insecure and become frightened when separated from a parent. They may regress and behave like a baby.

3 to 7 years Ward (1995) describes this as the 'magical thinking' stage. Children of this age are very egocentric. They believe that they are responsible for whatever happens. Those who are bereaved may therefore believe that they are to blame for the death. If this feeling is not explained, they will carry the guilt for the rest of their lives.

Children of this age can react casually to the news of the death but may ask about it at a later stage. Some children may believe that the dead person will return. Some will believe that they might die as well.

8 to 12 years At this age, children begin to realise that death is permanent. They also recognise that they will die one day. They may also feel resentful if there is less attention at the time of the death or immediately afterwards.

12 years to adult Teenagers understand the impact of loss and death but may not be emotionally prepared for it. As young people of this age are already experiencing a mixture of emotions, the response to death may be more extreme and variable than an adult's would be. As experiencing bereavement is usually unexpected at this age, friends may not have been through the process and may therefore be unable to offer support. Some adolescents experience depression.

Timetable implications of integration

There are many considerations to be given to the timetable implications of integrating pupils, particularly if there are several pupils with physical disabilities in a year group. Constraints include:
- grouping
- differentiation
- withdrawal support
- expertise of teachers.

There is frequently a 'trade off' between ensuring social integration and making the most efficient uses of resources, particularly in the funding of support staff.

Grouping

One group

Grouping pupils together in a class or tutor group, or a learning group, can ease the problem of making arrangements for support, especially if the pupils are always taught together as a group.

Several groups

Placing disabled pupils in a number of groups within a year band has benefits for social integration. Physically disabled pupils then have a wider circle of friends to mix with, and larger numbers of able-bodied students benefit from the integration process. This is a more expensive option, in terms of funding of support staff.

In sets

When pupils are set across a range of subjects in ability groups, timetable arrangements become even more constrained. There could be several pupils with physical disabilities in different areas of the school at the same time, doing the same subject. The timetable co-ordinator will need to consider whether availability of support staff allows for this, or whether some pupils will need to be in the same set, so that support can be shared.

Differentiation

Pupils with physical disabilities may not be able to participate in a particular subject, although this should be rare. For example, some pupils may not be allowed to do contact sports in P.E. An alternative arrangement will therefore be necessary for that pupil at such times.

At Key Stage 4, some pupils may not be able to cope with the full range of GCSE subjects due to medical factors. For example, pupils with muscular dystrophy tire very easily. The school therefore needs to find appropriate non-GCSE courses as an alternative, or in extreme cases, may need to consider part-time attendance.

Withdrawal from lessons

Pupils with physical disabilities are frequently withdrawn for physiotherapy, speech therapy and occupational therapy, in addition to any learning needs they may have. It is important that they do not miss too much of any one particular subject and that they do not miss any subjects where there is only one lesson per week, unless the school intends to disapply a pupil from a particular aspect of the National Curriculum.

In a school with several pupils with physical disabilities this can pose one of the most challenging aspects of timetable administration for the SENCO, balancing essential withdrawal support against the need to access the National Curriculum.

Distribution of teaching staff

Schools may wish to adopt a policy of all staff teaching all pupils, including those in withdrawal groups. The co-ordinator for the time-table will therefore have to integrate staff as well as pupils in the grouping arrangements. For example, a teacher of special needs may teach a GCSE set for English, whilst an English teacher teaches the language element of the Youth Award Scheme to a small number of withdrawn Key Stage 4 pupils.

Breaktime arrangements

A school which has pupils with physical disabilities may wish to make special arrangements to cater for pupils' needs at break and lunch times. For example, some pupils with disabilities may not be able to go outside in bad weather, due to the cold affecting their condition. Pupils with muscular dystrophy, cerebral palsy and chronic juvenile arthritis do not cope well with very cold weather and need to remain in the building. The following examples demonstrate how a school can make special arrangements for such pupils, although they are also of benefit to other pupils. It should not be assumed that all physically disabled pupils require such facilities. Rather, most pupils will want to access the usual range of activities on offer to all pupils.

Games room

The school may wish to provide a games area, which is available to pupils who cannot take part in active break pastimes. The area may provide activities such as table tennis, pool and board games. Such an area has the benefit of providing a 'haven' area for vulnerable pupils.

Pupils with physical disabilities could invite a friend to enter the area with them. Schools could operate a pass system for use of the facility. The area could be supervised if necessary. The area could be an adapted classroom. Resources – the equipment, the room, staffing – might be obtained through charitable means or via a bid from extra-curricular funds, should they be available.

Quiet area

Some schools provide an outside area which is designated as a 'quiet' area, free from boisterous activities. Pupils are expected to walk or sit in the area. With the provision of ramps and handrails, such a site could easily be adapted for disabled use.

Extracurricular clubs

Whilst the school should make provision for disabled pupils to have access to a range of extracurricular clubs, it may wish to make additional provision of sports for the disabled, either during a lunchbreak or after school. There are occasionally charitable funds available to set up and staff such clubs. It may be possible to make a 'cluster' arrangement, whereby all disabled young people in the area could attend, with joint funding by schools. Teams of disabled students could then enter regional and national disabled sports events, so that they compete fairly in their chosen sports. Sports especially suited to schools include boccia, polybat, wheelchair hockey, basketball, and swimming.

Personal care

Toilet arrangements at breaktimes will require consideration. Pupils may need a member of staff to help with personal care or may require extra time. Support staff hours may be necessary to cover such times, or medical staff could help by rota.

Meal arrangements

Special arrangements may need to be given to some pupils with physical disabilities, but only where absolutely necessary. Pupils with mobility problems may take longer to get to and from a school canteen. It may therefore be appropriate to allow pupils to go early to break or lunch. However, early arrival and departure for breaks and lunchtimes can sometimes be seen as advantageous by other pupils and resentment can occur if they feel it is not appropriate.

Use of assistants

Some pupils require help with eating arrangements. They may not be able to carry the food from the serving counter and may require an adult to help. Some pupils need a member of staff or an older pupil to cut up the food and feed them. Schools may therefore wish to allocate lunchtime as a part of support staff hours, or may use peer support for older pupils.

Use of additional facilities

Pupils should be consulted if they have difficulty with eating or require help. Most pupils are happy to eat with others if their personal care is handled sensitively, but the school may wish to consider providing a separate area if a pupil requests it. However, the social benefits of eating with others should not be neglected.

Allocation of additional time

In schools where breaks for eating are short, it may be necessary to allocate additional time for pupils with physical disabilities, or to alter the timing of the break. For pupils who find chewing and swallowing difficult it can take up to half an hour to eat a prepared lunch. They should be allowed to eat in an appropriate length of time and not feel rushed.

Movement about the school

Some pupils with physical disabilities have a fear of moving around school at the same time as other pupils, particularly if their previous experience has been in a small special school or junior school. Staff will need to take a flexible approach to how students can move around safely.

Flexible arrival/departure times

It may be necessary to allow a physically disabled pupil a few minutes additional time to get to and from lessons, either at breaktimes or between lessons. This alleviates the concern of many pupils that they will be caught up in a large crowd which may be moving quickly along corridors. Pupils who use lift access may also require additional time, especially if more than one child in the school requires such facilities.

Escort

Some pupils with physical disabilities benefit from the availability of an escort when moving around the school – for example, a sighted guide for a visually-impaired pupil. An escort could be either a class assistant or, for older pupils, a friend, who will help them to their destination. Care should be taken when allowing pupils to push wheelchairs however, and safety considerations should be taken into account.

Movement in the building

It may be necessary for the school to adopt a policy of one-way movement in corridors. This eases the 'flow' of pupils around the school and generally slows down movement, so that *all* pupils can move safely about the school. It is particularly important that pupils do not run in schools where there are physically disabled or visually-impaired children.

It may also be appropriate to restrict the speed at which a pupil may propel his or her wheelchair. Some powered chairs in particular can be very fast and would be dangerous if set at the top speed whilst moving between lessons for example.

School trips

The school should make a statement about pupils' access to trips in its equal opportunities policy.

When planning the trip, it should be assumed that all pupils in the appropriate age group will participate. Only in exceptional circumstances should a child be excluded. For pupils with physical disabilities this may be as a result of severe illness, for example, necessitating constant monitoring or nursing care.

When trips are organised, it is useful to make a list of all potential barriers to taking a disabled student, and then meeting each challenge in turn.

Prior to organising any trip from school, the organiser should visit the site. The following areas should be considered.

Insurance

Most schools have local arrangements for making insurance arrangements for trips out of school. It is sometimes necessary to inform the insurance company that disabled students are taking part in the activity.

Travel arrangements

If pupils use a wheelchair, specialist transport may be necessary. This may require the use of a school minibus for disabled pupils, or may require the hiring of transport. The cost of such facilities must be included in the total estimate for the visit. In many cases, parents may have their own adapted vehicle and may be willing to accompany their child on the visit. Some coach companies now have access for disabled people, including access for powered wheelchairs.

Staffing

Some disabled pupils require a high level of adult supervision. Staffing ratios may therefore need to be higher than usual.

Facilities

The site to be visited should be checked for accessibility, including ramps, lift access, number of stairs, space and toilet facilities. Although this can be checked with the site management staff prior to the visit, it is beneficial to take a disabled student on a pre-visit.

Accommodation

If the trip is residential, there are many considerations to be taken into account with accommodation. Access to the building is very important. If there is no lift access, the hostel or hotel staff may be prepared to accommodate a disabled student on the lower floor for example.

If access is not possible, the trip organiser will need to consider alternative accommodation, either for the whole group, or for a small number, so that the disabled student and a member of staff use adapted facilities nearby. Travel guides are now available which give information about access for disabled people, both in this country and abroad.

Adapted tasks

At present, not all sites and activities are accessible to disabled pupils. Course organisers will need to plan carefully for differentiated tasks and occasionally, visits, during a school trip. For example, walks may require adapting, so that wheelchair users have a flat even surface to travel on. If artefacts or displays are to be viewed, staff could arrange to bring them to the pupil, rather than trying to arrange for the pupil to move. Sighted guides can be used to describe items or views, and disabled students can be paired with physically able pupils to aid participation.

Outdoor pursuits need careful planning and adaptation. There are centres now available which cater for disabled people so that they can enjoy the full range of activities such as abseiling, climbing, sailing and horse riding. Such centres tend to be more expensive, but visits may be possible for small numbers of pupils, ideally in an integrated group.

It is possible to include pupils with disabilities in all activities, with careful planning, adapted tasks and a creative approach.

Chapter 2

Educational Implications of Disabilities and Medical Conditions

In order for schools to achieve successful integration of pupils with physical disabilities it is essential that there is an understanding of the special educational needs of each pupil, both for the relevance to planning for teachers, and for the impact on the attitudes of staff.

Medical labels are not always helpful in isolation for a child's learning difficulties, as there can be a very wide range of abilities within each condition. Additionally, many children have a combination of conditions and may have associated learning, psychological and/or behavioural disorders as well. For example, a child who is comparatively able-bodied may have quite severe learning difficulties associated with his or her condition, whereas a more severely physically disabled student may have no learning difficulties and may therefore require less support.

The attitude of the child and his or her parents should also be considered. Some pupils do not perceive themselves to be disabled and strive throughout their schooling to be as independent as possible. Others, who may have a less serious condition, may find it difficult to cope, are more dependent on adults and will require more pastoral and practical support.

Teachers need to be aware of the frequent overlap between medical, social, psychological and educational implications. Biological knowledge of a child's disability is, by itself, no guide to what the child may be like. It is also possible for staff to become overly fascinated in a medical condition so that the child as an individual is overshadowed by the disability.

It is therefore essential that the SENCO gains as much information as possible about the child in order to inform the staff. Such information can be gathered initially from parents, and with the pupil's carer, from other relevant agencies such as:

- hospital consultants
- GPs
- speech therapists
- physiotherapists

- social services
- special educational needs support services
- behavioural support services
- learning support services
- support services for visually and sensorily impaired pupils.

The information that most teachers need to know prior to teaching a child with a disability is:

- cause and description of the condition
- symptoms
- first aid, medical care and treatment
- educational implications
- personal care
- strategies for management in the classroom.

It would be possible to include some of the information in the individual education plan. One school presents the information in the form of a 'SNAPSHOT' (see Appendix 4), which is considered a main part of the individual education plan. Reference can be made to further information on the pupil's file. Information presented in this way on a single sheet of A4 paper is easily read and provides a concise summary of the pupil's needs. The sheet can be held by the class teacher in a primary school, or in subject department handbooks in secondary schools. Parents and pupils, where appropriate, can assist in the writing of the sheet. Such shared information results in a consistent approach throughout the school.

The following sections provide basic information and advice on making provision for pupils who have: spina bifida and hydrocephalus, muscular dystrophy and associated conditions, cerebral palsy, epilepsy, asthma, cystic fibrosis, spinal curvatures, limb deficiencies and visual impairment. Each section covers:

- Causes and description
- Symptoms
- Educational implications
- Medical care, first aid/health implications
- Personal/pastoral care
- Useful strategies.

Spina bifida and Hydrocephalus

Causes and description

The term spina bifida refers to a separation or split in the bones of the spinal column, exposing nerves. The physical consequences of the condition depend on the lesion and the amount of damage, which can occur at any point from the lower regions of the spine to the neck.

A large percentage of children with spina bifida also have hydrocephalus. This is a condition in which the ventricles in the brain are enlarged, as a result of obstructed flow of cerebral spinal fluid.

The causes of spina bifida and hydrocephalus are unclear, but are thought to include environmental and genetic factors. When a child with spina bifida has been born, the risk of a similar condition in further pregnancies is increased.

Symptoms

Children with spina bifida and/or hydrocephalus may have some or all of the following symptoms:
- total or partial paralysis in the legs
- paralysis of bladder and bowel
- poor circulation
- poor balance
- difficulties in upper limb tasks, poor fine motor skills
- visual impairment.

Educational implications

Learning difficulties

Some children with spina bifida will fall within the normal range of intelligence and will not require a differentiated curriculum. Others, particularly those with hydrocephalus, may have learning difficulties ranging from moderate to severe. In addition, absence from school may result in risk of poor achievement.

There is frequently a language problem present in that there may be a considerable difference between the verbal performance and intellectual ability. Such children appear to be fluent talkers, with language skills further developed than other areas of fine functioning. However, whilst speech may sound mature, it is often 'copied' and may mask an underlying lack of comprehension.

Concentration and motivation may be poor and many children require prompting to begin work and remain on task.

Eye conditions and visual difficulties can result in problems with depth vision. In such cases, children will be unable to distinguish figure from background, and may be unable to judge direction or distance.

Motor and spatial problems may also result in particular difficulties with number work and/or handwriting.

Medical care

Treatment

Children with spina bifida may require mobility aids such as callipers, a walking frame or wheelchair. Some children who can walk with callipers when young will require a wheelchair at secondary school age.

Children with hydrocephalus may be treated by the use of a shunt – a tube surgically inserted into a cavity of the brain which draws excess fluid to a safe area for disposal, usually the abdominal or chest cavity.

Bladder problems may be treated with the insertion of a catheter.

Pupils with spina bifida will require physiotherapy. They may also require occupational therapy and speech and language therapy.

First aid/health implications

Blocked shunt (drainage system to relieve hydrocephalus). Symptoms may present as drowsiness, lethargy, headache, appearance of squint. *Action:* refer to hospital/GP immediately.

Urinary infection. Symptom: increase in temperature. *Action:* refer to GP immediately.

Ulcers/painless fractures. *Action:* refer to GP immediately.

Personal/pastoral care

Pupils may need access to adapted toilet facilities and help with dressing. Younger pupils may require help with catheter changing. Pupils of secondary age should be encouraged to be independent in personal care needs.

Useful strategies

Pupils may require some or all of the following strategies.

Mobility

- Wheelchair access to school and classroom (see Chapter 4 'Resource implications').
- Seating near door for easy access to and from classroom.
- Flexibility of early exit/late arrival to lesson to avoid moving amongst large numbers of pupils in corridor.
- Peer support to collect items required for lesson.

Learning

Pupils may need access to:
- Multi-sensory teaching methods.
- Differentiated tasks and teaching methods.
- Use of support assistant as aid for practical tasks, amanuensis, interpreter.
- Tasks broken into smaller steps.
- Simplified instructions.
- Use of questioning by staff to ensure that the pupil has under-

stood the task (e.g. 'Now you tell me, what is it you have to do?')
- Access to information technology as an alternative means of recording work.
- Use of prompting to keep pupil on task.
- Special arrangements for exams – amanuensis, extra time.

Causes and description

Muscular dystrophy

There are over forty types of muscular dystrophies, which are all progressive, inherited neuromuscular disorders. They result in the breakdown of muscled fibre, and are defined as disorders of the motor units. Different disorders affect different levels of the motor unit. Some types affect both sexes but the most common form is Duchene muscular dystrophy which affects only boys.

Although muscular dystrophy is a genetic condition, it can appear in a family that has no history of it. Life expectancy of pupils with muscular dystrophy is limited and some pupils die in their late teens.

Symptoms

The main symptom of muscular dystrophy is gradually increasing muscle weakness as regeneration of the damaged muscles is not adequate and muscle is replaced by fibrous tissue and fat. The muscle weakness progresses slowly and there can be times of remission as well as rapid deterioration.

Educational implications

Learning difficulties

Most children with muscular dystrophy fall within the normal range of intelligence. However, illness may become more frequent in the later stages of the disease and frequent absence from school may result in poor progress. As the disease particularly affects hands and arms, handwriting and practical tasks may be affected.

Children who have rods inserted for improved posture are vulnerable if knocked. No contact sports can be played.

Medical care

Treatment

The nature of the condition means that all provision must include anticipated decreased mobility. In some cases, such progression may be slow, whereas in others, there may be rapid degeneration of muscle strength. There is no cure for muscular dystrophy.

Pupils may require the use of mobility aids at an early stage of the disease such as callipers and walking aids and as the condition deteriorates will require a manual or powered chair. Some pupils have metal rods inserted surgically in the back to help the child maintain an upright posture.

Pupils with muscular dystrophy will require physiotherapy on a regular basis.

Personal/pastoral care

Pupils may need help with all personal care needs as the disease progresses, eating, toilet arrangements and dressing for example. At later stages, one-to-one support will be required throughout the day – to greet the pupil and prepare him or her for lessons, to provide support throughout lessons and help with meal and breaktimes.

Reliance on support for personal care needs occurs during adolescence, at a time when most other pupils are becoming more independent; this requires sensitive awareness by all staff and careful consideration of pastoral support.

Most pupils are aware of their life expectancy. Counselling may be offered at any time, with parental consent, as a means of coming to terms with mortality. This may be offered by local support groups or by a national organisation such as CRUSE (see Section 'Useful addresses').

Useful strategies

Pupils may require some or all of the following strategies.

Mobility

- Wheelchair access throughout the school.
- Seating near the door for easy access to and from classroom.
- Flexibility of early departure/late arrival to class to allow for easy access in corridors.
- Support in class to access equipment and resources.
- Space for using mobility aid.

Learning

Pupils may need access to:
- Support assistant for class tasks. There is a need for a flexible approach. The level of support increases as the condition deteriorates.

- Differentiated tasks for practical activities.
- Careful consideration of the whole curriculum as the pupil may tire easily during the later stages of the disease.
- Special arrangements for exams – use of scribe, extra time.
- Access to information technology as an alternative means of recording work.
- Waiving of homework – pupils with muscular dystrophy become tired very quickly and may not manage to work at home after a school day.
- Sensitive handling of careers guidance.
- Bereavement education should be an integral part of the personal and social education programme, but consideration should be given to the class/tutor group if a pupil with muscular dystrophy dies during his or her school life.

Causes and description

Cerebral palsy

Cerebral palsy is a disorder which is caused by damage to a developing brain. Such damage can occur as a result of the following conditions: asphyxia (before, during or after birth), brain haemorrhage, malfunction of the placenta, or various illnesses such as meningitis, encephalitis, and jaundice.

The various forms of cerebral palsy are: *spasticity* – disordered control of movement, *athetosis* – frequent involuntary movements, and *ataxia* – unsteady gait with balance problems.

Symptoms

Children with cerebral palsy may have some or all of the following:
- Loss of control of movement, together with increased reflex activity.
- Restricted range of movement.
- Stiff and/or immobile legs.
- Quadriplegia or paraplegia.
- Poor head control.
- Poor speech articulation.
- Hemiplegia (one side of the body affected).
- Epilepsy, associated with cerebral palsy.
- Visual perception problems.
- Slow movement about the building (some children with cerebral palsy are prone to tripping, especially on stairs).

Educational implications

Learning difficulties

Children with cerebral palsy vary in ability, although a large proportion of pupils will fall within the normal range of intelligence and should therefore follow the mainstream school curriculum.

Children with a severe form of the disability may require augmentative communication devices, voice synthesisers for example, in order to access the curriculum. A major part of the curriculum may therefore involve teaching the use of the system, under the guidance of a speech therapist.

Medical care

Treatment

Treatment varies according to the nature of the disability. Most children require physiotherapy, using a programme structured by a physiotherapist. For pupils who use a wheelchair, there may be a need to spend some part of the school day in a standing position, using specialist equipment. In all cases, advice should be sought from the physiotherapy and occupational therapy department of the local health authority.

For pupils with impaired speech, advice and assessment should be sought from a speech and language therapist, so that a regular programme of speech therapy can be introduced. In many schools, such therapy is given by support staff, who consult with a speech therapist regularly.

Some pupils may be undergoing a programme of conductive education, which may have an impact on the school curriculum.

First aid/health implications

Approximately one third of children with cerebral palsy have epilepsy (see next section 'Epilepsy' for treatment and first aid implications).

Children with cerebral palsy are prone to falling more often as a result of their difficulties with walking and balancing, particularly on stairs.

Tiredness can also be a factor as children with cerebral palsy expend more energy than others due to lack of control of muscles and increased tone and movement.

Personal/pastoral care

Personal care needs vary according to the nature of the disability. Some pupils may require help with elements of dressing, whilst others may require one-to-one support at all times. Pupils with quadriplegia will require help with eating and with toilet arrangements.

Some pupils with cerebral palsy have low self-esteem particularly as they go through adolescence, and especially if they remain dependent on adults at a time when most others are becoming more independent. They may require additional help with confidence at this time.

Useful strategies

Pupils may require some or all of the following:

Mobility

- Wheelchair access to school and access areas.
- Seating near door for easy access to and from the classroom.
- Flexibility of early departure/late arrival to lessons.
- Additional time to move around the school.
- Seating at desk with ankles at right angles, resting on floor or foot block.
- Careful attention to seating on floor (pupils sit more comfortably on a chair in the correct posture).

Learning

- Support assistance, depending on severity of disability, ranging from help for practical tasks to full time one-to-one support, including personal care needs.
- Differentiated tasks for practical activities.
- Consideration of amount of walking, etc., on school trips.
- Special arrangements for exams – scribe, extra time.
- Access to use of information technology as an alternative means of recording work, together with alternative switch access.
- Use of adapted equipment to aid in practical tasks (see Chapter 4 'Resource implications').

Causes and description

Epilepsy

Epilepsy is a pattern of recurring seizures, resulting from brief biochemical changes in the brain. It affects children of all ages and abilities and is the second most common form of neurological disorder (migraine being the most common). Epilepsy cannot be described as either an illness or disease, but is a symptom of a physical disorder. There are various types of seizures: *tonic-clonic* – previously known as grand-mal, *absence* – previously known as petit-mal, and *complex partial, simple partial* and *sub-clinical*.

The causes of epilepsy are unclear, although it can occur as a result of an accident to the brain, cerebral palsy, infection, tumour or specific syndromes.

Symptoms

Seizures, or fits, are associated with:
- convulsions
- changes in perception and consciousness
- involuntary movements
- muscle spasms.

The symptoms may vary, according to the type of fit.

Tonic clonic   This type of fit may be typified by:
- crying out and falling
- stiffened muscles, which then relax
- convulsive jerks
- saliva round the mouth area
- loss of control of bladder and/or bowel.

Absence seizures   Typified by:
- apparent 'day-dreaming' – child staring into space
- fluttering of eyelids.

This type of seizure can be mistaken by staff as lack of concentration.

Complex partial seizures   Typified as:
- tic like movements, e.g. lip-smacking, plucking at clothes
- dazed, aimless walking
- periods of unresponsiveness
- confused behaviour.

These symptoms are sometimes mistaken for behavioural and/or emotional behaviour.

Simple partial seizures   Typified by:
- tingling sensation in arms or legs
- disturbance of feeling
- disturbance of senses, i.e. perception, taste or smell.

Sub-clinical seizures   Typified by:
- lack of attainment
- standard of attainment drops for no accountable reason.

Educational implications

Learning difficulties

Many children do not achieve their academic potential. The pupil may experience frustration and/or poor self-esteem as a result of the condition. Some pupils with epilepsy have brain damage and may have moderate to severe learning difficulties as a result.

Medical care

Treatment

Most children lead normal school lives as a result of medication which builds resistance to fits. Medication is usually taken at home.

However, some children who have tonic-clonic seizures may require the administration of medication in school, given by appointed staff at the discretion of the headteacher.

First aid/health implications

Staff should record all instances of seizures in school and inform the parents. In the case of tonic-clonic seizure, the following steps should be taken:

- The child should not be moved unless he or she is in danger.
- Allow the seizure to run its course.
- Loosen tight clothing.
- Place child in recovery position as soon as possible. Do *not* restrain child.
- Reassure the child as he or she regains consciousness.
- Remove child to rest area and allow to rest.
- Inform parents.

In rare forms of emergency, such as status epilepticus, rectal valium may need to be administered. In this case, the seizure shows no signs of stopping after a few minutes, or the child has a series of seizures without regaining consciousness. Such treatment should only be given where there are agreed procedures and by trained staff, with parental consent. These procedures can only be agreed at the discretion of the headteacher and staff. In schools where no such treatment may be administered, an ambulance should be summoned immediately.

Personal/pastoral care

Children with epilepsy who experience poor self-esteem may need extra help to overcome their difficulties. Time may need to be set aside to discuss how to build confidence.

If a pupil has a tonic-clonic seizure, he or she may lose bladder or bowel control during the fit. Sensitive handling of the situation is therefore required. It is useful for the school to request spare clothing to be used in such circumstances and to have blankets to wrap round the child following a seizure. This avoids any potential embarrassment.

Useful strategies

Pupils may require some or all of the following strategies.

Learning

- Discuss the condition with the class, to prepare for a possible fit during lessons.
- One-to-one support and supervision during swimming lessons.
- Differentiated curriculum as appropriate.
- Additional help to cater for any missed work.
- Head protector for pupils who have regular tonic-clonic seizures.

Asthma   Causes and description

Asthma is a physical condition which causes the airways in the lungs to narrow, making it difficult for the sufferer to breathe. Sudden narrowing of the airways produces an asthma attack.

Causes, or triggers of asthma, include allergies, exercise, cold weather, stress, excitement, viral infections and fumes such as exhaust, glue and paint. Asthma may also be inherited.

Asthma is one of the most chronic illnesses in childhood. It is manageable and large numbers of pupils take medication to school.

Symptoms

Asthma is characterised by some or all of the following symptoms:
- breathlessness
- wheezing
- repeated coughing
- tightness of the chest, accompanied by fear and difficulty with breathing.

Educational implications

Poorly managed asthma results in repeated absence from school which can lead to impaired performance.

Pupils with asthma fall within the normal range of ability and performance. The major effect of asthma on school life is inability to participate in physical education lessons, particularly in poor weather. Long periods of exercise are more likely to trigger an attack than short ones. Cold, dry weather can also exacerbate the condition.

Medical care

Treatment

Treatment for asthma is mainly preventative and/or relieving. Preventors such as Intal or low dose steroids guard against asthma and must be taken regularly. Relievers, such as Ventolin and Bricanyl are used when the symptoms of asthma appear. Most medication is inhaled. In extreme cases, steroid tablets may be prescribed for a short period.

First aid/health implications

All staff in school should be made aware of the symptoms of asthma and should receive training in case a pupil has an attack.

Pupils should be encouraged to take their medication as soon as symptoms occur. Pupils who have exercise induced asthma should use their inhaler *before* exercise.

In the case of an asthma attack, the following steps should be taken.
- Pupils should be reassured and encouraged to calm down. They should rest before resuming the activity.
- If symptoms worsen or do not reduce, medical attention should be sought.
- In severe cases, an ambulance should be summoned.

Personal/pastoral care

Pupils with asthma may experience frustration associated with their condition and may require additional support from their class teacher or tutor to cope with this. They should be encouraged to become as independent as possible in the use of their medication.

Useful strategies

Pupils may require some or all of the following strategies:
- Allow pupil extra help and time to catch up on missed work.
- Encourage independence in use of medication in school, to avoid attacks.
- Give access to differentiated curriculum/tasks for physical education, if appropriate.

Cystic fibrosis

Causes and description

Cystic fibrosis is a genetic disorder which produces thick mucus on the lungs and pancreas, resulting in cysts. The mucus causes lung infections and prevents enzymes in the pancreas, which digest food, from flowing to the intestines.

Rarely, there are associated conditions, such as diabetes, arthritis, heart condition, cirrhosis of the liver, sinusitis and hay fever. Boys with cystic fibrosis may have delayed sexual maturity.

Cystic fibrosis is a life threatening condition. The average survival is almost thirty years.

Symptoms

Cystic fibrosis is characterised by:
- persistent coughing
- wheezing
- failure to gain weight
- chest infections.

Educational implications

Children with cystic fibrosis should be able to lead a full and normal school life, participating in all activities. Some children experience behavioural and/or emotional difficulties associated with their ability to cope with the condition. The condition frequently results in a child needing hospital care, resulting in the possibility of school work being missed.

Medical care

Treatment

Children with cystic fibrosis require enzymes, which must be taken with all food. Older pupils may need to carry portable intravenous equipment about the school. Occasionally nebulisers are required and courses of antibiotics may be prescribed to combat infection.

First aid/health implications

Children with cystic fibrosis can be prone to chest infections and prolonged bouts of coughing, during which they may cough up mucus or vomit.

Daily physiotherapy is essential in order to clear the lungs. This may occur before and after school, but is sometimes necessary in school time. Schools will need a trained member of staff who can carry out the treatment, usually a support assistant.

For pupils who require intravenous treatment, arrangements will need to be made in consultation with the headteacher, parents and staff who are willing to supervise.

Personal/pastoral care

Children with cystic fibrosis may require additional pastoral support in order to help them cope with the frustration often experienced due to the condition. If behavioural problems occur, effective behaviour management strategies should be outlined on the individual education plan.

Staff will need to liaise frequently with the physiotherapist and GP in order to monitor the treatment required in school.

Useful strategies

Pupils may require some or all of the following strategies.

Learning

- Extra help and time to catch up on missed work.
- Provision of school work during absences.
- time for daily physiotherapy to clear lungs.
- Supervision of medication at meal times if pupils are young or unable to be independent.
- Special arrangements and extra time for exams.

Causes and description

Spinal curvatures

There are three main types of spinal curvatures: *scoliosis, kyphosis* and *lordosis*. Scoliosis results in one hip being higher than the other and one shoulder blade being more prominent. Kyphosis is a posterior curvature of the spine, resulting in affected lung capacity and shortened stature. Lordosis describes a forward curvature of the spine as viewed from the side.

Spinal curvatures are usually caused by congenital or neuromuscular disorders, such as spina bifida, cerebral palsy or muscular dystrophy. They can also develop as a result of tumours, infections and metabolic diseases.

43

Symptoms

Children may have the following symptoms:
- shortened stature
- pain associated with the condition
- decreased lung capacity
- altered posture.

Educational implications

Some pupils with spinal curvatures require hospital treatment. They may therefore miss a lot of school work.

Many pupils with this condition experience pain and may tire easily as a result. Some pupils are not able to take part in any physical activity.

Medical care

Treatment

Some pupils with spinal curvatures are directed to wear a body brace or jacket to correct the posture. In severe cases, corrective surgery may be advised. This could involve the fusing of some vertebrae and/or the insertion of metal rods which maintain a more upright body posture.

First aid/health implications

Pupils may be prescribed pain-killing medication, which may need to be administered in school. There may also be a need for a rest area if pupils tire easily.

In severe cases, pupils should not be involved in boisterous play. The availability of a breaktime area for quiet leisure activity may be an advantage to such children.

Personal/pastoral care

Pupils with spinal curvatures may suffer from low self-esteem linked to their perception of body image, particularly if a body brace or jacket is worn. Staff should be aware of the potential for others to tease such pupils and offer additional pastoral support to increase confidence.

Useful strategies

Pupils may require some or all of the following strategies.

Mobility

- Adapted physical education programme or disapplication from physical education.
- Flexible approach to arrival and departure time to/from lessons as the pupil may require additional time to travel about the school.
- Access and adapted seating arrangements to cater for posture difficulties.

Learning

- An adapted curriculum to cater for the needs of a child in pain, and who may therefore tire easily.

Causes and description

Limb deficiencies

Pupils may have partial or total limb deficiency, which can be congenital or acquired. The cause of congenital limb deficiency is not known, as only a very small percentage shows a hereditary link. Since the drug thalidomide was banned in the UK, no drugs have been shown to have the effect of preventing growth of limbs.

Acquired limb deficiency occurs as a result of surgery, accident or disease.

Educational implications

Pupils with limb deficiency may have poor or slower mobility about the school. They may find using stairs difficult. In some cases, limb deficiencies can affect the body's ability to control fluid balance ad temperature, resulting in high fever and absence from school.

Medical care

Treatment

Some pupils are fitted with artificial limbs. Depending on the type of deficiency, a wheelchair, crutches or walking aids may be used.

First aid/health implications

Staff will need to be aware of the risk of minor infections developing into a high fever.

Personal/pastoral care

Pupils with limb deficiencies should be encouraged to be as independent as possible. However, younger children may require help with skills such as dressing, personal independence skills and toilet arrangements.

As pupils get older, there may be difficulties with low self-esteem, relating to self image. There may therefore be a need for additional pastoral support to help the child cope with the condition.

Useful strategies

Pupils may require some or all of the following strategies.

Mobility

- Seating near the door for easy access to and from the classroom.
- Flexibility of early departure/late arrival to lessons.
- Adapted seating, if required.
- Use of lift/stair lift if necessary and available.

Learning

- Access to support staff for help with practical tasks.
- Allowance of extra time or help to catch up on missed school work.

Visual impairment

Causes and description

Many pupils have minor visual problems which can be effectively treated by the use of training or lenses. However, for some children, damage or developmental anomalies occur, resulting in more serious conditions of visual impairment.

Visual impairment is related to dysfunction in the eye, relevant nerves or part of the brain. Blindness is a symptom of visual impairment which is either partial or total. It may be congenital or acquired.

There are three main categories of impairment: *malformation* and *inherited disorders* including cataracts, defects of the iris; *acquired eye disorders* including accidents, resulting in retinopathy or prematurity;

brain disorders, congenital or acquired – for example, brain tumours, hydrocephalus, trauma, congenital malfunction of the brain. Visual impairment can be associated with other disabilities, such as hearing impairment, cerebral palsy and epilepsy.

It is vital that the SENCO receives full advice and support from the visual impairment services and consultants, as individual pupils' needs vary considerably.

Symptoms

Symptoms of visual impairment include:
- loss of clarity (acuity) resulting in blurred vision
- loss of visual field
- loss of colour vision
- sensitivity to light
- near or short sightedness.

Educational implications

Many pupils have minor visual problems which can be effectively treated by training or the use of lenses. However, for some children, damage or developmental anomalies occur, resulting in more serious conditions of visual impairment.

Pupils may have some or all of the following difficulties:
- *learning difficulties* – 80 per cent of learning is through visual channels;
- *social difficulties* – pupils may experience difficulties in new situations, may not be able to use non-verbal communication, may have difficulty in making new friends;
- *reading* – including focusing problems, slow reading speed, inability to read small print, to scan, to read from board, to share books;
- *close work* – difficulty with drawing tasks for example;
- *writing* – inability to hand write, read back work, see lines on paper;
- *mobility* – pupils may experience difficulty in moving in a crowded environment, or may be unable to take part in some forms of physical activity.

Personal/pastoral care

Pupils with visual impairment should be encouraged to be as independent as possible. They may need additional pastoral support in order to cope with possible frustration experienced as a result of their condition. In particular, social skills may need to be sensitively handled.

Useful strategies

It is very important that professional support for the visually impaired is sought by the SENCO in order to offer the best possible strategies in school. Such support agencies include local education authority visually impaired service teams and health authority consultants, who can offer a wide range of resources and advice to teachers.

Pupils may require some or all of the following strategies:

Environment

- Well lit areas.
- Blinds to cut glare from windows.
- Consideration of floor surfaces, e.g. change of surface to identify an area.
- Highlighting of stair edging.
- Hand rails on ramps, slopes.
- Signs to identify areas of the school.
- Lift access to different levels of the school.
- Low level displays.
- Consideration of fire exit routes.
- Use of aural clues to identify areas.
- Spacious corridors/classrooms.
- Seating near exits and at front of room.

Staffing

- Use of trained, sighted guide.
- Use of support staff as amanuensis, interpreter, etc.
- Good use of voice control – voice easily identified by pupils.
- Consideration of clothes, e.g. providing good background for possible signing.

Learning

- Seating near teacher or demonstration.
- Large print books and worksheets.
- Low level vision aids, e.g. magnifiers, as advised by health authority staff or peripatetic teachers.
- Differentiated tasks to cater for variable concentration, ability to work.
- Differentiated worksheets with clear, uncluttered layout, good contrast, clear print and background, non-shining paper, description of diagrams.

Figure 2.1 Information technology: use of scanner for pupil with visual impairment.

- Alternative means of recording work (see Chapter 5 'Differentiation').
- Special arrangements for tests, exams – extra time, use of amanuensis, large-print papers.
- Braille adapted equipment.
- Thermo former/stereo copier, to make tactile diagrams.
- Information technology equipment, as advised by peripatetic staff.

Chapter 3

Individual Education Plans

Individual education plans (IEPs) are now a recognised part of a SENCO's documentation. They were introduced by the DFEE in 1994 to help teachers plan in consultation with parents, and are intended to provide a structure of planning and evaluation for pupils with special educational needs. Available to students at Stage 2 or above, a good plan will provide students and parents with comprehensive targets for all aspects of development.

IEPs will also contain a summary of provision, reviews and evaluation procedures, together with outcomes of reviews. The plan should include the following information:

- The nature of the child's difficulties
- Action taken by the school
  - provision
  - resources: staffing implications
  - resources: specific, i.e. programme/activities/materials/equipment
- Targets
- Parental support
- Pastoral care/medical requirements
- Monitoring and assessment arrangements
- Review arrangements and dates.

The IEP should differ from the pupil's record and should be used as an action plan rather than a retrospective review.

Local education authorities and individual schools differ in their response to the management of IEPs. Some local education authorities have a prescribed format, although schools may develop their own if they wish. In primary schools, the plan may be written by the class teacher in consultation with the SENCO. In secondary schools each subject teacher is expected to contribute to the plan, which is co-ordinated by the SENCO.

When considering IEPs for pupils with physical disabilities, it may not be necessary to complete details for all subjects of the National Curriculum as the IEP should reflect only those targets which *are different* to those for all pupils. For example, it may be that a pupil requires different resources in practical tasks, such as during Technology or Art, but has no different targets in English or Humanities. In such cases, the IEP may refer to a few subjects only.

The format of IEPs varies between schools. IEPs work best when the amount of paperwork is kept to a minimum, giving essential information and gaining contributions in an efficient way, so that all staff who teach a pupil feel able to make valuable contributions. In a primary school, the IEP may be developed on a single sheet of paper, whereas in a secondary it would be possible to collect targets and reviews from each relevant member of staff, pupils and parents, and then collate the information on a small number of pages. An example of such a process is given in Figure 3.1.

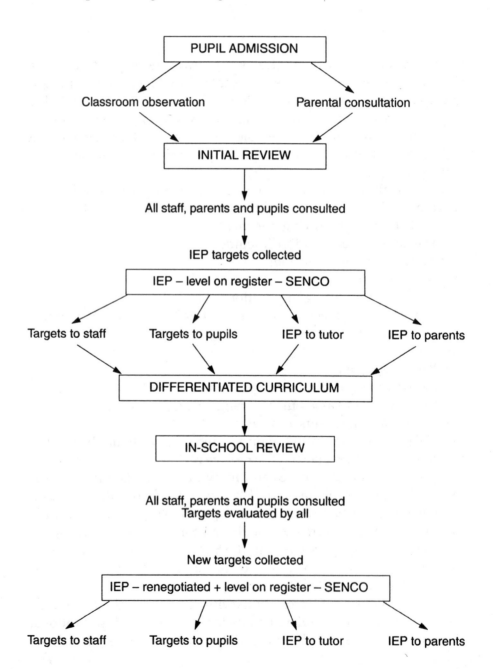

Figure 3.1: A possible format for the process of writing and evaluating an individual education plan.

Nature of pupils' difficulties

It is essential that staff who teach a pupil with disabilities are aware of the general and specific difficulties with learning and access to the curriculum. The IEP should state the exact nature of the disability in a concise way, together with the educational implications. For example, some pupils with disabilities may have difficulties with practical tasks only, whereas others may have learning difficulties associated with the condition which affect all areas of school life.

Schools will need to consider which terms they may use in their section of the IEP.

Such information given on an IEP gives the teacher a very brief outline of the disability and the likely educational implications. Further information is kept on pupil records and can be referred to if necessary. An example of such a statement in this section of the IEP might be:

> Charlotte has cerebral palsy which has severely affected her mobility and speech. She is able to participate in all lessons. She needs additional time to make her responses. She will need to use her laptop to present written work. She needs the support of a classroom assistant for practical tasks.

This section of the IEP will probably not change throughout the pupil's time at school. It therefore needs careful consideration and can be written in consultation with parents and the pupil (depending on age), on admission to school.

Action – special education provision

This section of the IEP should detail the provision made by the school in terms of staffing and resources, and should describe any programmes which are different to those followed by the majority of pupils.

Provision

For pupils with disabilities, it is necessary to consider whether the child will follow the total school curriculum, including the National Curriculum. Some pupils, for example, may not be able to participate in physical education, or some aspects of it, and may therefore need to have alternative provision listed on the IEP.

In some instances, physiotherapy, speech therapy, occupational therapy and hydrotherapy are offered in school and the actual sessions or times of such support should be listed on the IEP. Charlotte's IEP may therefore now be added to in this way:

> **Provision**
>
> - 1 session of physiotherapy per week – 30 minutes, Monday 11.10am.
> - 1 session of speech and language support per week – 45 minutes, Thursday, 2.20pm.
> - 1 session hydrotherapy – 1 hour, Tuesday, 2.20pm.
> - Occupational therapy – as requested by school. 1 visit per term.
> - Access to in-class support, shared, 5 hours per week – Technology, Art.

If Charlotte had learning difficulties in addition to her physical disability, then withdrawal for individual teaching or small group work, together with the actual time, may also be added.

Again, this information may not change during a year.

Resources/staff implications

The IEP should indicate any additional staffing allocated to a pupil, together with the type of staffing support offered. For example, whether the speech and language programme would be followed by a classroom assistant under the direction of a speech therapist, or whether there is an available speech therapist for all sessions. Similarly, whether physiotherapy is undertaken by support staff, under the guidance of a physiotherapist, or whether the pupil sees a physiotherapist regularly.

SENCOs will need to state if learning support is shared or individual or whether teaching support is offered, and how it is arranged. There is a difference between 1 hour teaching support for individual work, and 1 hour ancillary support, shared between 4 pupils. Parents need to know exactly what their child is to be offered by the school.

The special needs budget is variable across authorities but it might be useful if SENCOs considered how support is allocated across the continuum of the special educational needs register. There should clearly be a recognisable increase of support for pupils who are on higher levels of the register. Charlotte's IEP may therefore have the following section:

> **Staffing allocation**
>
> - Tutor   – additional pastoral support 20 minutes per week.
> - Speech therapist – 1 session per week – 40 minutes.
> - Physiotherapist – 1 session per week – 40 minutes.
> - Class assistant – 5 lessons – shared with 1 pupil – 5 hours per week.

Resources/materials and equipment

The IEP should list the actual resources required by the pupil in order to access the curriculum. Such resources may include whole school resources, such as use of the lift or stair ramps and use of an adapted minibus. They may also include smaller items which may be available in class, such as laptops, computer access, writing desk, pen grips, foot rests.

Under this heading, there may also be a reference to any differentiated materials or tasks that will be offered to the pupil. In some instances, differentiated text may be all that is required. For example, a pupil with visual impairment may require text in larger print.

Examples of the type of equipment that is available for pupils with disabilities are listed in Chapter 4 'Resource implications'.

This section of 'Charlotte's' IEP may now include:

Materials/equipment

- Use of laptop computer to record work.
- Differentiated tasks for P.E.
- Adapted cutlery and non-slip mat for meal times.

Targets

Targets described in an IEP should be SMART targets. That is, they should be:

    Specific
    Manageable
    Achievable
    Realistic
    Timed

Targets show exactly what the pupil needs to achieve during the period of the IEP. They should be 'specific objectives in observable learner outcomes terms, from which specific teaching strategies can be derived' (Norwich 1995). They should, where appropriate, relate closely to the statement of special educational needs.

Ideally, targets should be devised in consultation with the pupil and should be monitored regularly. The termly review of pupils on the special educational needs register is the ideal time for this, although the evaluation of progress towards targets should be ongoing. Pupils and parents should receive a copy of the IEP, including specific targets. If pupils are able, they should also monitor their progress.

Examples of IEP targets for pupils with physical disabilities might be:

- To increase the speed of word processing to 40 words per minute.
- To use a scanner on at least five occasions during the week.
- To gain a certificate for wheelchair proficiency.
- To learn how to play polybat (an adapted version of table tennis).
- To practise working with an amanuensis for pieces of writing over half a page.
- To swim ten metres, using a flotation aid.
- To use a dictaphone for homework tasks.
- To learn to print work from a laptop.
- To use five phrases on an electric communication device per term.
- To change a catheter independently.
- To make two oral contributions per lesson.
- To complete one session of physiotherapy per day with an assistant.

Personal/pastoral care

Pupils with physical disabilities who are integrated in a mainstream school very often require additional pastoral care, particularly as they get older when self-esteem can sometimes become an issue. The IEP should specify a key member of staff who can be responsible for managing the pastoral care of the pupil.

Additionally, pupils with disabilities sometimes require medical and/or personal care, which needs sensitive handling. Details of such requirements are given in Chapter 4 'Resource Implications'.

Chapter 4

Resource Implications

Whole-school environment

Environment

The DFE circular 6/94 stated that: 'It is clearly desirable that a spectrum of mainstream schools should be fully accessible to the disabled'. Regulations now require that local education authorities and the funding agency for schools provide regular information to the DFEE on the accessibility of school buildings for pupils with physical disabilities.

The major problem for many schools is that buildings are old and do not provide immediate accessibility, especially for pupils who use wheelchairs. In a study completed by Coopers and Lybrand for the National Union of Teachers (Coopers & Lybrand 1992), it was found that 46 per cent of primary schools could provide access to 75 per cent or more of their teaching space. Secondary schools could provide such access in only 18 per cent of schools. However, the study also concluded that the costs of progressing integration were not particularly high, with the exception of start up costs for major conversions of buildings.

Information now required by the Secretary of State includes:
- whether the school is completely accessible to pupils who use wheelchairs;
- whether the school is partially accessible and, if so, what percentage of teaching space is available;
- whether there are adapted toilet facilities which are accessible to pupils in wheelchairs.

For schools that do not currently have access, there is a grant available, to which schools can bid via the local education authority or, for grant maintained schools, via the funding agency for schools. All *new* building work, however, must now have access for disabled people.

In some authorities, schools have 'clustered' provision, whereby a primary and secondary school makes provision within a local area for a specific type of special educational needs. One school for example may have resources for pupils with sensory impairment

57

whilst another may have provision for pupils with physical disabilities. This may provide a short-term solution to integration, in that schools could be adapted one by one. Ideally, however, all schools should be considering how they could adapt their existing buildings to provide access.

In some cases, this may require adaptations to rooms, so that some parts of the school can be made more accessible. If so, the timetable could be rearranged so that disabled pupils require less movement about the school. Coopers and Lybrand found that one primary school in the survey had reorganised all the classes which one of its pupils needed to attend so that only the ground floor of the building needed to be used. Partial accessibility may be seen as a necessary step towards full access.

Many schools may need to provide toilet facilities which have to take into account the additional space required for a pupil to manoeuvre in and out of a wheelchair. Consideration must also be given to the amount of space required by a pupil, a chair and possibly, up to two members of staff or a hoist, should the pupil require lifting from his or her chair.

John Bangs (1995), suggested that schools should carry out an audit of provision for their current buildings, using the following review questions:

- What are the existing spaces which are already accessible for pupils with physical disabilities?
- How many floors are there which are accessible for pupils with physical disabilities in the school's buildings?
- Which areas can be made accessible within the school's budget?

Adaptations to buildings can be categorised as either higher or lower cost. Higher cost specifications are generally more permanent.

High cost adaptations
   New buildings or extensions.
   Installation of lifts.
   Toilets for disabled pupils.
   New toilets for disabled pupils.
   New changing rooms.
   Stairmate.
   Stairlift.
Lower cost adaptations
   Adaptation of existing changing areas.
   Adaptation of existing toilet facilities.
   Installation of hand rails in toilets, playgrounds and areas where there are steps.
   Installation of ramps to entrances and class areas, with side protection rails.
   White edging on stairs.
   Provision of fireproof doors on upper floors.
   Provision of additional lighting in corridors.
   Reinforcement of bases on doors.

Portable stairclimbing wheelchairs are now available which require no building adaptations and can be operated independently. They require no lifting or transferring of pupils (see Wheelchair Corporation Ltd in the 'Useful Addresses' section).

Schools may not need to provide all of the above modifications. It is very beneficial to carry out an audit with a disabled pupil, who has the ability to highlight any problem areas in the school.

It is worth noting that when a disabled pupil has access to upper floors of a school, fire safety will become an important aspect of the health and safety policy. Some schools have a fireproof zone on upper floors which allows the pupil and a member of staff to wait in a safe area for the fire brigade. Other schools may use specialist stretchers or wheelchairs that can be wheeled up and down stairs. In any event, lifts may not be used as a fire escape route.

Coopers and Lybrand concluded that the costs of further progress in integration are not particularly high. Many smaller modifications will enable access for a larger number of pupils with physical disabilities. Frequently, the provision of access can be linked to the attitude and willingness of the school to integrate.

Class environment

A flexible approach should be taken to the management and organisation of classroom areas, so that pupils with physical disabilities can be integrated as easily as possible. Provision includes the following considerations.

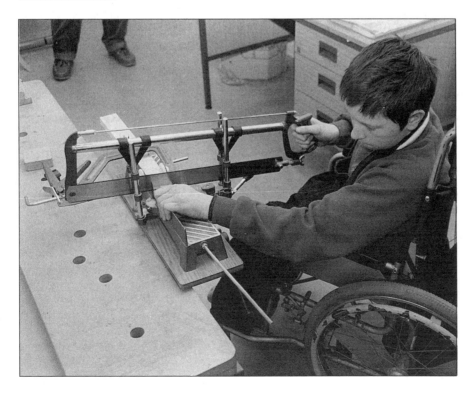

Figure 4.1 Access – pupils using wheelchairs require space to move around equipment

59

Space

Careful attention needs to be given to the arrangements of seating and work areas. Pupils with mobility problems who may additionally use wheelchairs require extra space to move to and from desks and to move about work areas.

Seating

Pupils who have mobility difficulties need to be seated by the door to the classroom, so that they can leave the class early or late if necessary. This also reduces the need to move about the whole class area.

Children with physical disabilities need to sit near equipment, to reduce the amount of movement about the room.

Additionally pupils with visual impairment will need to sit at the front of the class, near the board or displays.

Work areas

Pupils who use wheelchairs require variable height work surfaces, including desks, benches, sinks and cooking facilities. They may also require additional surfaces for technology equipment such as portable computers, tape recorders.

Displays

Each teaching area should have low level displays and image boards so that pupils who use wheelchairs or who have visual impairment can benefit from them.

Lighting

Pupils with mobility problems and some pupils with visual impairment require well-lit areas to work and move about in. In some cases, pupils with visual impairment cannot tolerate glare and blinds may be necessary to provide the correct environment.

Equipment

There is a vast range of equipment available for pupils with physical disabilities. Examples are given in the section headed 'Equipment', in Chapter 5.

The number of special needs support staff in mainstream schools has risen steadily over the past few years. Effective management of such staff can be the key to successful integration for pupils with physical disabilities.

Staffing

The SENCO should give consideration to the following areas when employing support staff, who could be teachers or non-teaching assistants.

- The needs of the pupil.
- Timetable implications.
- Job descriptions.
- Induction for new staff.
- Planning for support.
- Provision of relevant information.

The needs of the pupil

Most pupils who require additional adult help will have an individually designed education plan. The needs of the pupils should determine the amount and type of support required. Some pupils with more severe disabilities can be fairly independent and not require a great deal of assistance, whereas others may have a combination of less severe disabilities and rely heavily on adult support. The amount of support may also vary according to the age of the child. It is hoped that most pupils become more independent as they get older. In general, primary aged pupils can be happy to work with the same adult for much of their school time. This is not so evident at secondary age.

There needs to be a flexible approach in determining the amount of support required. For example, the SENCO should be prepared to respond quickly if a child with a medical condition deteriorates rapidly. Similarly, as children mature or become more confident, support may be withdrawn.

In planning for support the SENCO clearly needs to liaise with parents and the pupil, in addition to considering current levels of resources in the school.

Timetable implications

A creative and flexible approach to the timetable implications of integration is vital, since pupils with physical disabilities require a wide range of support provision. In extreme cases, a pupil may need one-to-one support at all times. Other pupils may require a high level of shared support, whilst another group may require support for specific teaching areas.

The timetable for support staff will be largely determined by the number and ages of the pupils with disabilities. If there are only a small number of such pupils in the school across a range of year groups it may be more difficult to provide shared support. In schools with more than one physically disabled pupil in a year group, who may be grouped together for teaching, support can be shared. It should also be noted that the availability of support for a physically disabled pupil can benefit other pupils with special educational needs in the same classroom, especially if a child is being 'weaned' away from total dependence on an adult helper.

Timetabling of support can be achieved in several ways.

Tracking a pupil or class

In this method, one support assistant follows a named pupil or a class of pupils throughout their school curriculum. The main advantage of this is that a pupil can establish a good relationship with one adult over a period of time. Knowing the pupil well can help the assistant learn the best way to give the pupil access to the curriculum. This method is often used in primary schools where it is more likely that individual pupils are named as requiring a set number of hours of support, and an adult is employed to provide it.

Working with a year group

The SENCO might decide to allocate a special educational needs support assistant to each department or year group within the school. It would then be necessary for the head of the subject or year to allocate the support across the curriculum according to need, in consultation with the special educational needs department.

The advantages of this are that the support assistants would work closely with the teaching staff in one subject only and would gain more knowledge of a specific curriculum area. They would also become more familiar with lessons as they spend time in the same department.

The disadvantages of this system are that it assumes that heads of departments are familiar with all the needs of the special educational needs pupils and are able to prioritise according to need. It also assumes that at any given time a pupil will require support in their subject. It does not cater for the fact that there may be several other pupils in other subjects whose needs are more urgent on that particular occasion. In general, pupils with physical disabilities require more support in practical tasks, resulting in an imbalance of support in these areas. If five lessons of Technology are being taught at the same time in a large comprehensive school, for example, it may be possible that there are five pupils requiring support. Those same five pupils may not require help in English.

However, it is more effective if the same support assistant can support pupils in each of their subjects, for example in all three Science lessons through the week.

Matching the need to the support

This is the most time-consuming and complicated but most effective means of supporting pupils with physical disabilities. The SENCO needs to identify all the times in the day when a pupil most requires support. This may be during practical work, such as Physical Education and Technology, or for written tasks. This exercise must be repeated for all pupils who require support. After an evaluation of that process, staff are allocated according to their expertise and the priorities. It is beneficial if support staff are distributed according to their strengths. In a secondary school, for example, it is easier, although not essential, to support a pupil in Modern Languages if there is some prior knowledge.

This method has many advantages. Children are supported on a priority basis, rather than the availability of staff. Support staff time is not wasted. For example, in some instances children are allocated ancillary hours and if the same person supports the child they may well be with a pupil at a time when they are not most needed. By matching need to support, individual lessons throughout the week can be allocated with support.

The flexibility of this system means that support staff do not need to be in a whole lesson. With prior planning, it may be agreed that he or she is only required for the written tasks, or for practical help with changing for a Physical Education lesson, before going to another class.

Role of support staff

In general, staff who support a pupil with physical disabilities need to have a highly flexible approach in their management of the pupil. Their role can include, one-to-one support work, small group work, whole class work and observation.

One-to-one support

Such support should be allocated only to a pupil who has severe physical disability, such as the later stages of muscular dystrophy or more severe forms of cerebral palsy involving the whole body. Supporting such a pupil may involve providing help in communicating and the recording of work.

Aiding communication
Some pupils may not be able to communicate orally. They may use an augmentative communication device, such as the liberator Light Talker or Delta Talker, with which a pupil selects symbols or words using a switch access device. Alternatively the pupil may use a specialised symbol system as directed by the speech and language

therapist. Support staff may be required to help the pupil in such use, under the direction of the teacher or speech therapist, following a set programme. They may also devise alternative means of recording work using the system, following lesson plans provided by the teacher.

Recording work

Some pupils with poor motor control may require an amanuensis who can write down their responses to a task. Support staff may be used to act as such a scribe. It is important that training is given so that it is the pupils' responses only which are given.

Support staff can also offer physical assistance in manoeuvring a mouse for example or helping with word processing. Where pupils use a dictaphone to record work, staff may need to operate the machine.

Support in practical tasks

Support staff have an invaluable role in offering help to a physically disabled student during practical activities such as Technology, Music, Art and Physical Education. Support can take many forms, including holding equipment steady whilst the child is working, guiding a pupil's hand when using, for example, a saw or a bat,

Figure 4.2 Support staff – help in practical tasks

helping to control equipment whilst a child is on task. Supporting the child in the water during a hydrotherapy or swimming lesson or acting as a partner in Physical Education may be necessary. Specific examples of the use of support staff can be found in the following section.

Acting as reader, interpreter, prompter

Some pupils may require all written information to be read to them. This will be necessary if the pupil has impaired vision or a disability which results in poor co-ordination or posture. For pupils who have impaired speech and language processing skills, the support staff may need to interpret the information in a more simplistic form so that the child can understand the content. Such information could be presented in the form of symbols or pictures, and this work could be prepared by the class assistant.

In some instances pupils benefit from being prompted. Pupils with spina bifida in particular may need this type of help, which sets them on a task and helps them to maintain concentration.

If the school intends using such support for end of Key Stage tests or for examinations, the pupil should have access to that form of support in lessons. Both the pupil and the support assistant need to work regularly with each other so that the pupil has the best opportunity to achieve his or her potential.

Assisting with personal care needs

Some pupils with physical disabilities require a high level of support for personal care. This includes help with toilet arrangements, dressing and personal hygiene. Such support should always be sensitively handled but this is especially important in adolescence. Pupils need to feel confident and as relaxed as possible and support staff need to be adequately prepared for the role. Class assistants may be required to lift pupils from their wheelchairs to a toilet, change continence pads, deal with menstruation, dress or change a pupil for Physical Education or swimming, wash a pupil after a meal time and keep the pupil free from excess saliva. All of these roles demand calm and efficient handling with the minimum of fuss. The health and safety policy should always be followed. Where bodily fluids need to be dealt with, procedure and disposal should follow agreed guidelines in order to avoid risk. It should also be emphasised that wherever possible, manual lifting is not performed in schools. Rather, a hoist should be provided. Where manual lifting is unavoidable, staff should be given training in safe lifting techniques and should lift in pairs, with another adult.

Assisting with physical care

Pupils with physical disabilities who require one-to-one support also frequently require regular physiotherapy, speech and language therapy, occupational therapy and/or hydrotherapy. Class assistants frequently help in the provision of such programmes, especially if for example, the physiotherapy needs to be undertaken on a daily basis. In many cases, a physiotherapist will determine the programme of work to be followed and a member of the support staff will supervise the child through each session. Similarly an assistant may follow a language programme as set by a speech and language therapist.

Some pupils may require time out of their wheelchair for reasons of comfort, and may either need to rest or to be upright in an aid such as a stander. It is often the task of the support assistant to help in physically supporting the pupil at such times.

It should always be remembered that support staff should work under the direction of a teacher or therapist. Their role is to support and enable the pupil to access the school curriculum, following programmes which are planned by the teaching staff and support professionals.

Small group work

In most instances, the support staff's role is to provide shared help to a small number of pupils. This can occur in or out of the classroom, under the direction of the teacher.

In-class support
Support staff may have a number of pupils to help in any one lesson. This may take the form of practical help, such as drawing tables, grids, or in reading and interpreting the task to a number of pupils and keeping them on task.

Withdrawal support
Staff may be asked to take a small group for an activity outside of the classroom. This may be for the purpose of following a speech and language therapy programme, or supervising computer aided learning for example. In such cases, the programme of work should be set by the teacher or therapist.

Observer
The benefits of lesson observation cannot be overestimated. Teachers can make good use of support staff by occasionally asking them to observe a lesson without intervening. Observation can serve to give information to a teacher about: teaching style, the pupils' ability to access the work, the pupils' ability to remain on task, the social interaction between pupils and the behaviour of pupils. Observing staff

will require guidelines and a prepared observation sheet, detailing exact methods of recording.

Management of Support Staff

Effective management of all staff is a significant factor in the successful integration of pupils with physical disabilities. It is very important that support staff in particular have equal status in the school, in the eyes of both staff and pupils. It is therefore necessary to ensure that such staff have equal access to in-service training, induction and appraisal systems, where appropriate, and that they are a part of the staff care programme of the school.

Induction

Support staff frequently commence work within days of appointment. This may be partly due to funding issues, or as a result of decisions made during annual reviews. It is therefore particularly important that the school has an agreed induction programme for new staff. The programme should include:
- Meeting with the immediate line manager.
- Provision of the school handbook. It may be useful to have a department handbook for support staff, with all relevant extracts copied into it.
- Provision of the school's special educational needs policy.
- Period of observation with another member of the support staff team.

Training/staff development

As support staff become more confident, they should be encouraged to attend courses which are relevant to their work. These may include first aid or medical issues, aspects of special needs such as behaviour management, supporting pupils with learning difficulties, information technology. Some authorities offer qualifications such as the Certificate of Applied Professional Studies.

The school programme should also allow for development of support staff in the form of regular in-service training, which is additional to whole-school issues. Areas such as paired reading, special arrangements for exams, working as an interpreter could be covered. Such training should be specific to the school's needs.

Chapter 5
Differentiation

The National Curriculum gives entitlement to all children to a broad, balanced, relevant and differentiated curriculum. Whilst the aims of the school should be the same for all pupils, teachers must find the different means by which pupils can achieve them. Such a process allows for a flexible approach to teaching methods, resources and learning activities, based on individual needs.

There are many ways in which tasks and equipment can be adapted to improve access to pupils with disabilities. Such differentiation should be planned as part of the individual education programme. What follows is a section outlining some possible strategies for differentiation areas, beginning with some ideas on information technology and alternative means of recording work, which is common to all written tasks. The list is by no means exhaustive. Many of the strategies have been found to be successful and have arisen from consultation between the pupil and the teacher.

Other strategies include use of support staff, adaptation of the environment, differentiated tasks and some examples of specialist equipment. In some subjects, examples of adapted lessons are given.

Information technology

There is currently a vast range of software and hardware available in education and there is little doubt that information technology can address some additional needs of students with physical disabilities. Information technology can help students to:
- Communicate, using voice synthesisers.
- Write at length, using word-processing programmes and predictive phrase packages. These are especially beneficial to students who find writing by hand very difficult, or who tire easily.
- Gain access to the Art, Technology and Music curriculum, with computer-aided design programmes.

Alternative means of recording work

- Record and monitor science results, using sensors and tools which can be attached to computers.
- Draw diagrams, graphs and tables.

Access to information technology

Schools will need to take several factors into consideration when providing information technology for students with disabilities.

Creating access

A major factor is the placement of the information technology equipment in school and whether the area is accessible to disabled children. If the equipment is portable, will the child be able to carry it around the school if necessary? In some secondary schools portable information technology equipment is available in each department, thereby preventing the need for pupils to carry valuable and sometimes heavy loads in busy corridors.

Not all class areas have readily accessible plug sockets, or if they do, the disabled pupil may find himself or herself isolated from the rest of the group whilst working alone in a corner. There is an advantage in using portable computers in this situation as the equipment can be run on batteries, although cost needs to be taken into account.

Students who use wheelchairs will require a variable-height work place so that they do not strain muscles or sit in an uncomfortable position whilst working at a computer. Adapted seating may be necessary for other children.

For pupils who have visual impairment, lighting in the teaching area will be very important as the screen may reflect light back or appear too dull.

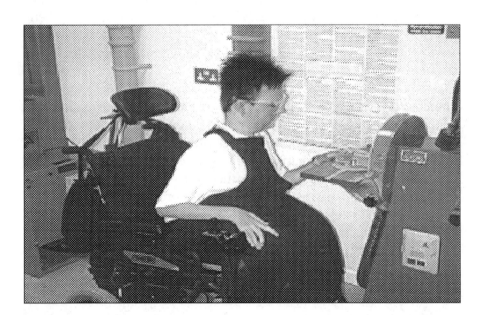

Figure 5.1 Access – variable-height equipment improves access

Specific adaptations

Keyboards

There is now a wide range of keyboards available. Disabled pupils may prefer to use large or expanded versions which are compatible with standard computers. Tilting the keyboard may help to improve access.

Some pupils prefer to use keyguards – a piece of metal or plastic which fits over the keyboard with holes over the keys. These prevent the wrong letter being pressed. Children whose hand movements are not steady may particularly benefit from this adaptation.

An alternative means of helping pupils who have weak or unsteady arms is to use an arm or wrist support which allows the arm to rest during word-processing. The support can also move in the direction of the user's arm as he or she works.

For pupils who can only use one character on the keyboard at a time there are 'sticky key' facilities, which lock the shift key on one press and unlock it on another. This is useful for pupils who use only one hand or an aid such as a head pointer.

As advances in technology are being made at such a fast rate, it is advisable for the SENCO or Information Technology co-ordinator to contact specialist services in order to obtain the most effective means of keyboard access (see section 'Useful addresses').

The use of overlay keyboards can also benefit disabled pupils. A paper overlay is placed over the top of the keyboard and when the pupil presses an area the computer reacts to the message. Most programmes now offer access via overlay keyboards, which can be divided into any number of areas from two to two hundred. They therefore benefit all ages. Large areas are particularly suitable for children who do not have fine movement control. Increased amounts of text can also be assigned to areas, so that pupils do not need to type out individual letters or words. This may be of benefit to younger disabled children.

Mouse

All mice work in the same way – a ball underneath the mouse moves a cursor around the screen and selections are made by pressing the mouse button. Mice can be adapted for disabled children. In some cases, they are simply enlarged or operate in reverse – that is, the mouse remains still and the student moves the roller ball, which is on top. Mice can also be adapted to be operated by a foot. In some cases, the button action is replaced by a switch, which can lock temporarily.

Movement of the mouse can vary according to the surface it is on. The use of mouse mats can slow down the movement if necessary. Mouse speed can also be altered by additional access facilities, or through control panels on the computer. The speed required to 'double click' on the mouse can also be changed.

The range of available options is generally found in current information technology catalogues (see section 'Useful Addresses').

Touch screens and switches

For students who find the use of a mouse or keyboard difficult, touch screens may provide a solution. Touch screens allow for the student to use a head or a pointer directly onto the screen. The current disadvantage of this however, is that small or precise areas of the screen may be difficult to locate. Cost may also be a disadvantage, as the system needs to be calibrated for each individual student.

Switches can be one of the easiest methods of accessing computers. They are available in all shapes or sizes; therefore whichever part of the body is best controlled can be used to operate the computer. Some students, for example, use head-activated switches on pads either side of the head, chin-switches, or foot-operated switches. Programmes being used need to be switch accessible. Most switch access programmes work on a scanning principle. The choices are usually presented in grid form and the indicator scans across and down the rows. The student activates the switch and the required letter or icon is selected. Such programmes can range from very basic to extremely sophisticated, thus enabling access to pupils of all ages. However, switch access is much slower than keyboard or mouse access.

Use of sound

Computers can be voice activated. Students who are unable to use switches, but who can speak, can make sounds into a microphone in order to operate software.

More sophisticated voice input systems can act on commands. It is anticipated that work in this area will rapidly develop.

Communication devices

Some pupils with physical disabilities are unable to communicate, for example, pupils with quadriplegic cerebral palsy. They may have poor muscle control which prevents them from using signing systems.

There are many different speech aids and they all operate on the same principle. The student selects text or icons, and the message is converted to speech by the computer. Speech can be in different languages and accents. It can be related to age and can be a male or female voice, to suit the needs of the individual.

For young children, or pupils who have associated learning difficulties, the simplest speech systems have pictures which activate a message. At a more sophisticated level, using a machine such as the deltatalker, icons can be combined to produce complex messages.

The computer can be mounted on a wheelchair for easy accessibility, and can also be activated using switch access.

Speech synthesisers can be used by the pupil selecting letters to enter text, which is then read out.

Such augmentative forms of communication allow for physically disabled students to take a full part in school life.

Being informed

In order for disabled students to access information technology in school, it is necessary for staff to be informed about how the equipment is to be used and how to maintain it.

Information technology equipment and especially adapted equipment for disabled pupils, is a major expenditure outlay for a school. Wrong decisions can be very expensive. It is advisable therefore to seek advice on the appropriate equipment for individual children. There are several specialist services which carry out individual assessment and give advice to schools (see section 'Useful addresses'). In addition, most authorities have specialist advisers or special school staff who may have used suitable software or hardware, or who may even be able to provide it to individual pupils. There is also funding available for information technology use from some charitable organisations.

Schools may wish to consider training staff in the use of the facilities, possibly alongside the pupil, so that the information can be shared with colleagues. Such training may be essential for support staff who work alongside individual pupils.

Access to technical support is also essential. Some schools may wish to work together in this area, each contributing to the purchase of information technology technician support which can then be shared. Some secondary schools have their own technician who may be able to support the disabled pupils and help to maintain equipment.

There are may courses available to staff on the subject of information technology, together with information technology exhibitions. Many of these are particularly beneficial in that they frequently offer the opportunity of using the equipment and programmes.

There are many ways that a school can adapt the environment to cater for physically disabled pupils, in addition to the building adaptations listed in Chapter 4. However, the debate about adaptation of environment should also be considered. That is, should the environment be totally adapted for a disabled pupil, or should the pupil be taught to cope with the environment? The following adaptations might be made.

The environment

School environment

- Floor surfaces – level, clearly defined changes in surfaces, anti-glare.
- Portable ramps.
- Blinds to cut glare.
- Well lit corridors.
- Windows – low level for pupils in wheelchairs.

- Hand rails.
- Low-level displays.
- Doors, floors, walls with good, clear contrast, and non-glare surfaces.
- Highlighting on stairs, door handles, switches.
- Clear labelling to identify areas, cupboards.
- Changing facilities for disabled.

Class environment

- Well lit areas.
- Blinds to cut glare.
- Space, to allow for wheelchair access around desks, benches.
- Lack of 'clutter' – no excess furniture or equipment.
- Variable-height desks, work surfaces, benches, machinery, sinks.
- Low level displays and image boards.
- Highlighting on steps, cupboards, switches.
- Clear labelling to identify areas of the room.
- Ramps – to allow access to fixed equipment, areas of room.

Tasks

When considering differentiation, it is useful for the teacher to identify the *essential* learning outcomes of the lesson and then plan the means by which disabled pupils can achieve those outcomes. The advantages of such differentiation are clearly not limited to disabled pupils. They will benefit many pupils within the class, including those with learning difficulties. For an example of breaking down learning outcomes in a lesson to what is essential, desirable and possible, see Appendix 5.

Such planning may include the use of the following strategies:

- *Cloze procedure.* Allowing the pupils to use one or a few words whilst others are writing in complete sentences or paragraphs, for example.
- *Cut and paste tasks.* Sentences or paragraphs are given in printed form. The pupil arranges them in order and pastes them into their book.
- *Multiple choices.* Ringing words or numbers, or choosing the number of the answer, allows for less writing or the use of an augmentative communication system.
- *Pre-prepared tasks, results, grids.* These can be provided on paper, disc or in a separate drive on a network. The pupils simply record results and answers, rather than spending time on drawing grids and tables. This increases the likelihood that pupils will complete tasks.
- *Provision of taped information.* Some pupils may require repeated information or instructions. The provision of information on a cassette linked to headphones can enable the pupil to learn more independently. Audio cassettes can also be used for 'talking

Figure 5.2 Differentiation – paired with an able-bodied student

books' for visually impaired pupils.
- *Provision of recorded lesson.* Some pupils benefit from having the teacher input recorded on video or cassette. The information can then be used at home or separately in the classroom.
- *Pairing with physically abled student.* This allows pupils to work more independently of staff and enables appropriate sharing of paired tasks, e.g. the physically abled student can carry equipment, draw tables.
- *Increased scale of experiments.* In Science, for example, the use of larger amounts in experiments give more demonstrable results, e.g. where colour differences are required, visually impaired pupils will benefit from more obvious changes.
- *Careful planning when movement is required.* For example, a 'circus' of experiments or displays can be arranged so that there is minimal movement for a pupil with mobility problems.
- *Use of demonstration equipment.* Teacher demonstration equipment is frequently much larger – for example, children's reading books, ammeter, stop clock. Such equipment can be used by the pupil.
- *Change of rules.* Rules of games can be adapted to match the needs of physically disabled pupils. Examples are given in Appendix 6.
- *Adaptation of task.* For example, in gymnastics, if the task is to learn how to do a forward roll, the task may be adapted for a physically disabled pupil so that a rocking movement is performed; or, if a wheelchair is used, a reverse wheelie balance is

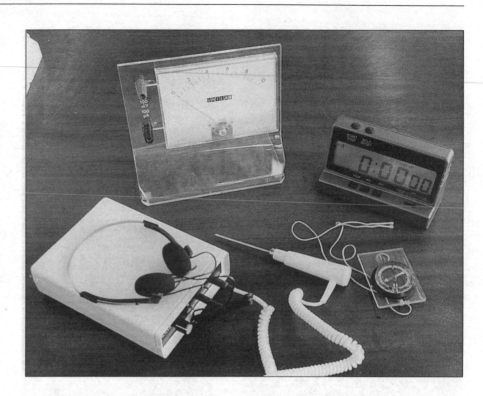

Figure 5.3 Differentiation – use of demonstration equipment

substituted for a roll. For orienteering skills, the route may be shorter and routes more clearly highlighted. During a table tennis lesson, pupils may play the 'polybat' version – a recognised sport for the disabled.

- *Individual programme.* In some instances, the pupil may require a separate task. During a residential trip, for example, if access is not possible, an alternative activity may be arranged. If pupils are not able to do contact sports, an alternative individual skills lesson may be planned.

Figure 5.4 Playing Polybat – an adapted version of table tennis

- *Use of computer-aided programme*. If pupils are requested to draw or design for example, a computer package may be used to aid a physically disabled pupil. An example is 'Corel Draw'.
- *Use of pre-prepared 'kits'*. For example, in Technology, kits or patterns for designs can be provided for physically disabled pupils to follow and make. Science equipment may be pre-assembled.
- *Increased teacher direction*. Teachers may guide some pupils more than others – for example, to suggest the best method of performing practical work.
- *Modified equipment*. See the following lists for specific subjects.

General to all lessons

Equipment

For many pupils with physical disabilities, access to the full curriculum can be aided by the use of specialist equipment. There is a wide range of equipment available in catalogues, but frequently, the best adaptations are those which have been designed for individual use. Many schools have used technological knowledge and enthusiastic do-it-yourself experts from amongst parents or from other sources.

The following lists summarise some of the most useful equipment that can be used in subject lessons, commencing with a list of general equipment that could be useful for all subjects. They are not intended to be exhaustive, as new products are constantly being developed.

Written tasks

- Computer + appropriate software, e.g. predictor programmes
- Word processor
- Dictaphone
- Audio cassette
- Hand/pen/pencil grips
- Dark-lined paper

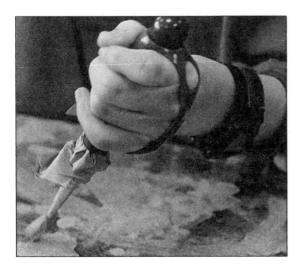

Figure 5.5 Equipment – use of handgrip

77

Reading tasks

- CD–ROM
- CD–ROM with speech
- Talking books
- Scanner
- Low vision aids, e.g. magnifiers, reading lamps

Specialist equipment

Mathematics

- Raised edges on desk/trays – to prevent items falling off
- Large dice
- Electronic dice
- Large-button calculator
- Talking calculator
- Braille adapted equipment, e.g. protractor, ruler, clock
- 3D shapes
- Specialist scissors – for one-handed use

Science

- Digital thermometer
- Talking thermometer
- Large-button calculator
- Talking calculator
- Non-slip matting
- Hand grips – to hold apparatus (Figure 5.5)
- Braille adapted equipment, e.g. tape measure, ruler, clock
- Demonstration equipment, e.g. large ammeter, voltmeter, stop clock
- Range of data logging equipment, connected to computer for large displays, easy reading
- Video microscope
- Specialist scissors – for one-handed use

Food Technology

- Pull down shelving
- 'Grabber'
- Talking thermometer
- Adapted cookers, voice microwave ovens
- Specialist clock for visually-impaired pupils
- Multi grips – to hold cutlery, utensils
- Easy-grip handles
- Mouldable handles – for cutlery, utensils, etc., designed to mould to individual pupils' hands

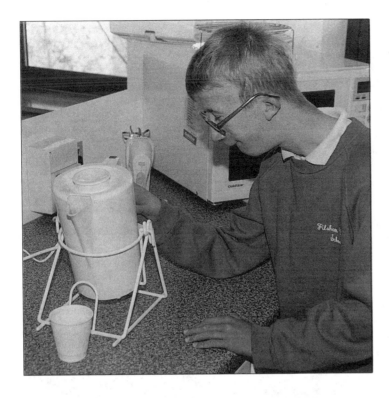

Figure 5.6 Equipment – pouring

- One-handed aids
- Pouring aids – for kettles, dishes (Figure 5.6)
- Cutlery guides – for disabled pupils to cut and slice
- Autochop – for chopping with one hand
- Specialist knives
- Cutlery board with spikes – to hold food steady
- Tap turner – for use by people with poor muscle strength
- Non-slip mats, surfaces
- Specialist scissors – for one-handed use

Technology – resistant materials/graphics

- Converted stool to accommodate Hegner fretsaw (Figure 5.7)
- Peg store to hold components, e.g. for soldering
- Device for holding nails – students who cannot grip can then simply hit nail
- Mitre saw – particularly useful as student needs only one hand to operate it – the work is kept at a right angle throughout
- Grid papers – for line work
- Pre-drawn border paper
- Non-slip matting to keep work steady on surface
- Computer-aided design packages, e.g. 'Design View', 'Publisher', 'Draw'
- Light box – students with visual impairment can trace, rather than draw
- Portable sander – good for pupils with mobility problems as less

Figure 5.7 Equipment –
converted stool to
accommodate Hegner saw

movement around the room
• Specialist scissors – for one-handed use

Physical Education

• Polybat equipment – bats, wooden struts
• Foam equipment – balls, javelin, discus
• Velcro gloves, bats, racquets
• Football with lead shot fitted – rattles for visually-impaired pupils
• Kickmaster football – has a retractable cord
• Specialist buoyancy aids for swimming
• Boccia equipment – balls and ramps (Figure 5.8)
• 'Floater' ball – lightweight and slower movement
• Cloth coloured balls
• 'Spider' balls – rubber legs prevent ball from rolling away
• Shuttleball equipment – adapted version of badminton/tennis
• Indoor hockey set – lightweight ball and sticks
• Dressing aids
• Shower chairs – can also be used to wheel disabled child into swimming pool

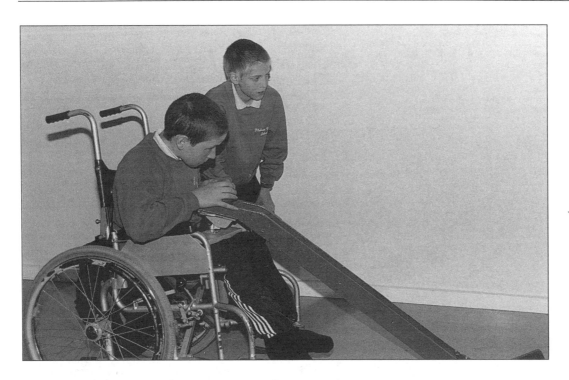

Figure 5.8
Equipment –
playing
Boccia

Figure 5.9 Equipment – use
of batting tee

Examples of Lesson Plans for Science and Physical Education

All teachers should be responsible for meeting the needs of pupils with special educational needs in their classes. It is important therefore that provision is carefully planned. One method of planning for differentiation is to write the main lesson plan and then consider a range of strategies to meet the needs of individual pupils, within that framework. The following examples demonstrate how this may be achieved.

Basic lesson plan
Daphnia Heart Rate

Year 10 – Science

Context of the lesson

The group will have done work on circulation and maybe even already have seen the heart rate of water fleas (*Daphnia*). They will be working on the nervous system and the effects of drugs, with the next part of the syllabus being a move to hormones. This lesson is an attempt to show the safest of very low doses of chemicals on the heart rate of water fleas and therefore also on our own heart and nervous system.

Aims and learning outcomes

Skills:
* To reinforce, extend and practise microscopy skills.
* To reinforce, extend and practise scientific AT1 skills of: Predicting, Obtaining Results, Handling Results (Tables/Averages, etc.), Evaluating Results (Concluding/Criticising, etc.).

Theory:
* Reinforce the need for a pump even for a 1mm organism, to aid diffusion.
* Heart rate responds to chemicals.
* Stimulants (Caffeine) and depressants (Alcohol).
* Introduce Adrenaline.

Time line (Lesson plan) Based on one hour and 30 minutes lesson – Lesson 1

Time	Teacher	Classroom assistant if available
2	Introduce the water flea and demonstrate safe working practice for viewing under the microscope using minimal cotton wool. Instruct them to focus and find the heart.	Listening and watching (unless previously briefed to other tasks)
7	Helping focusing. Reassuring that they have heart rate	As teacher
17	Praise group for finding heart and discuss problem of counting heart of such a fast beat (approx 180/minute) (Done best using video microscope). Using student to tap out heart beat of theirs/demo tapping technique.	Listening and watching (unless previously briefed to other tasks)
22	Instruct to take 3 readings and average them for their water flea. Then help them to do so.	As teacher
32	When a few have done this gather group round to demonstrate other chemicals. Predict as group (show of hands) what might happen if we give the water flea coffee or 'get it tipsy' alcohol. Then demonstrate how to add to daphnia safely.	Listening and watching (unless previously briefed to other tasks)
37	Instruct to change each chemical and repeat readings as before. Aid progress of lesson. Question and ask about fair tests as appropriate.	As teacher
52	Warn to finish.	Aid those most behind
55	Tidy and clear up.	Help clear away
60	Praise group. Collect a full set of results on the board. Brief discussion. Then instruct to evaluate own results, using the board ones to fill in the gaps of those missing.	Helping with presentation to anyone needing it
68	Aiding and questioning while the students are working on own mainly.	As teacher

Apparatus and equipment

Microscope	15
Slides	100
Absorbent cotton wool	some
Large mouthed or cut off plastic droppers	15
Stop watches	15
Waterfleas in pondwater small beakers	15 beakers
0.5% Alcohol	5 multiples of 20ml
0.1% caffeine or 1/10 strength normal coffee	5 multiples of 20ml
0.01% Adrenaline	5 multiples of 20ml
Video microscope if available	1

Risk assessment

Chemicals are in very low concentrations so minimal risk. See Hazcard for adrenaline. Emphasise care for animals and safe working practices. Otherwise normal lesson procedures.

84

Differentiated lesson plan

Daphnia Heart Rate

Context of the lesson

As normal lesson plan but catering for various types of students.

Students	Differentiation strategies	Advantages for rest of class
Visually impaired	Use of video microscope. Able bodied student operates the microscope. Partially sighted can watch the television screen and do tapping. (Waterflea will take up full screen.) Assistant describing teacher instructions and waterfleas, etc. Use of computer for results and writing (as can be blown up larger). Prepared table. Large size available, so they do not need to see board. Assistant aiding practical skills if required, although this should not be needed.	Video microscope can be used to point out heart, show techniques and other interesting things that come up such as a pregnant one, to whole class. Video microscopes are one of the best investments for a science department.
Wheel chair user	Microscopes are a problem due to position so again use video microscope with pairing of able bodied student. Chemicals, etc. accessible. Otherwise as per normal.	As above with video microscope. Frees up any assistant for the rest of the class once started.
Motor control problems	As with wheel chair user. But able bodied student will need to perhaps do more of practical aspects on health and safety grounds. (Check risk assessment.) Prepared tables for results. Use of laptop or class computer, with table prepared on disc to save time and allow them to get on quickly and to type their results. Use of Excel (spreadsheet programme) for averages and graph drawing. Then, if required, assistant or teacher help.	As above with video microscope. Frees up any assistant for the rest of the class once started.
Associated learning difficulties	Prepared tables for results. Diagram instructions with a flow chart available. Proforma with guidance questions available for the write up. Taking the class results for use with the write up. Differentiation by outcome as to level of AT1 write up. More care and reassurance regarding explanation of what is required. Use of laptop or class computer, with table prepared on disc to save time and allow them to get on quickly and to type their results. Use of Excel (spreadsheet programme) for averages and graph drawing. Then, if required, assistant or teacher help.	This is the group that will most need help, however anything prepared for this group, such as diagrammatic instructions or a table on the computer will also help absentees, late arrivals due to music lessons, students who find it difficult to listen to instructions.
Dyslexia, handwriting or spelling difficulties	Use of laptop/classroom computer to write up the evaluation. Again this could be on proforma identical to that for the rest of the class already saved on disc. Spell check, etc. before printing.	A second copy can be printed for absentees.

Other factors needing consideration

Pace of the lesson according to ability (possible extension activities for some, e.g. graphing results). Level of work covered.

Basic lesson plan

Athletics

Context of the lesson

Aims and learning outcomes

- To introduce sprinting technique
- To introduce common root throwing skills

Time line (Lesson plan) Based on one hour lesson – Lesson 1

Time	Teacher	Classroom assistant if available
5	Introduce warm up – 'cones and clues' – students run to spaced apart cones and find clues to a well known personality.	Aid with dressing and moving to area
2	Stretches – full body.	As teacher – suggesting differentiated stretch routine for some
10	Organise groups of 3. Introduce sprinting task – 1 timer, 1 runner, 1 marker. Ask 'How far can you run in 6 seconds' – each pupil repeat x 2	Working with disabled pupils
15	As above – 1 runner, 1 observer, 1 timer. Observe partner's technique, using check sheet. Advise partner and repeat run to see if any improvement.	One-to-one with disabled pupil or group
5	Organise pairs – Introduce task and demonstrate.	
20	Take it in turns to throw different objects.	Retrieve object if necessary.
	Ask – 'How does throwing action change?'	Aid with dressing/mobility

Apparatus and equipment

Stop watches

Cones

Footballs

Hoops

Quoits   } to throw

Tennis balls

Bean bags

Risk assessment

Safety very important during throws
- well spaced apart
- throw on command
- collect object
- no running
- do not throw object back
- place object down

Differentiated lesson plan
Athletics

Year 7 – Physical Education

Students	Differentiated strategies
Visually impaired	• Work alongside sighted guide or pupil • Work as timer – counting seconds allowed • Use specified route – highlighted with markers
Wheel chair user	• May need help with dressing • Ensure cones are accessible – on level ground • Place clues near top of cone for access • Stretching of upper body – working alongside peers • Chair race – could race against other wheelchair users • Consider technique for manual chair users – body position, etc. – use of different check list for observer • Depending on upper body strength, may need foam objects/small objects to throw, or use batting tee or ramp to propel object.
Motor control problems	• May need help with changing • Differentiated stretching programme, depending on need • Have one set of clues/cones in smaller zone for easier access • Time against self, so no differentiation for running task • Use of foam or smaller objects for propelling • Consider teacher advice according to disability, e.g. wider base, adapting arm action, two-handed throw • Ask able bodied student to retrieve objects if necessary.

Appendix 1

**Medical Sheet
Information on: Asthma**

Description

A condition in which the airways in the lungs narrow.

Symptoms

Often worse at night
- coughing
- tight or 'heavy' chest – people describe the feeling as 'a large elastic band round the chest'
- whistling noise or wheezing
- breathlessness

Treatment – First Aid

Asthma attack
- Administer reliever (inhaler) quickly – as directed
- Administer reliever again if no improvement after 10 minutes
- Encourage pupil to stay calm – take deep breaths
- Encourage pupil to sit with hands on knees
- Encourage pupil to slow down breathing

If no improvement
- Call ambulance or medical assistance

Appendix 2

Medical Information

NAME: JOHN SMITH   **YEAR:** 10   **TUTOR GROUP:** BD

| Medical Condition | Spinal Muscular Atrophy

| Complications | Cannot cough and needs treatment immediately if choking

| Symptoms |

- Pupil is distressed.
-
-

If you notice any of the above symptoms, take the following immediate action.

- Class assistant to administer immediate treatment as per training.
- If symptoms persist, *Emergency medical procedure* – send message to reception, and ask for 999 call to first aider – give room number.

- This pupil should have adult supervision at all times.

Appendix 3

Medical Information
Medical Information **Daily Log**

DATE: 28.04.97

PUPIL'S NAME: John Smith

COMPLAINT: Hit head hard on floor

TREATMENT: Ice pack on bump

               Checked for concussion

               Parents informed

SIGNED:

DATE:

PUPIL'S NAME:

COMPLAINT:

TREATMENT:

SIGNED:

Appendix 4

Snapshot

NAME: CHARLIE   **YEAR:** 7——

NEED TO KNOW:

Charlie has Duchene muscular dystrophy. He uses a powered wheelchair. He has very little muscle strength.

EDUCATION IMPLICATIONS:

- Charlie tires easily and may not manage afternoon lessons in mainstream.
- Charlie will have one-to-one support in all lessons.
- Charlie will require adapted tasks.
- All written work will be with an amanuensis.
- Charlie will attend hydrotherapy and physiotherapy.

USEFUL STRATEGIES:

- Planning time with ancillary support staff to differentiate work.
- Less reliance on written tasks.
- Use of variable-height equipment.

STRENGTHS:

Charlie is a very personable young man with a great sense of humour. He always tries his best.

* ADDITIONAL INFORMATION ON FILE *

CENTRE LINK: Ms_____

Appendix 5

**Differentiation:
Learning Outcomes – Technology**

What you have to do

All students will:
- Write a clear design brief.
- Draw and label a range of ideas.
- Develop ideas by drawing and writing about how the design will be made.
- Produce a final drawing, in isometric projection and rendered.
- Plan how the product is to be made by drawing a simple flow chart.
- Produce a materials list.
- Evaluate the design.
- Follow the plan carefully to make the product.
- Evaluate the product – what worked and did not work, what needs changing, is it successful, is the product like the design you set out to make.

Some students will:
- Write a clear design brief.
- Write a specification.
- Develop ideas by discussion, drawing and writing about how the product will be made.
- Produce a 3D coloured drawing of the design proposal.
- Produce a simple orthographic drawing with some help.
- Draw up a materials list.
- Draw up a work plan that lists all stages and all tools to be used at each stage.
- Use more complex processes, like the lathe.
- Follow the plan carefully to make the product.
- Evaluate the product – what worked and did not work, what needs changing, is it successful, is the product like the design you set out to make.

Some students might:
- Write a clear design brief.
- Write a specification including ergonomic considerations and anthropometric data.
- Discuss and draw a range of ideas.

- Produce exploded drawings of the design.
- Produce a fully coloured and detailed drawing in 3D, adding realism to the drawing.
- Produce a complete orthographic drawing, to scale or full size, showing all measurements.
- Draw up a work plan that lists all tools and materials, and make notes when having to change it because of difficulties.
- Use more complex processes, e.g. lathe, computer for lettering, CNC milling machine, card developments.
- Follow the plan carefully, checking the design and modifying it (and recording changes) when things go wrong.
- Produce an article that is indistinguishable from a real working model, including high quality finish and detail.
- Evaluate the product, saying whether or not it is fit for the purpose – what worked and what did not, what parts needed changing and why, is it like the original, suggest improvements, ask others for their opinions.

Appendix 6

| **Differentiation:**
Physical Education – Adaptation Of Rules |
|---|

Defending:

Physically abled players may not:

- Defend the ball when possessed by disabled player. They may only defend the area (i.e. basketball, netball).
- Have contact with disabled player (i.e. football, rugby).
- Pick up a ball hit by a disabled player until an agreed number of seconds have elapsed (i.e. cricket, rounders).

Attacking:

Disabled players may:

- Travel with the ball for an agreed number of seconds before being tackled (i.e. football, hockey).
- Carry the ball, rather than bouncing, dribbling, etc. (i.e. basketball).
- Have additional time/bounces to return ball (i.e. volleyball, tennis, table tennis).
- Throw ball, rather than hit it (i.e. tennis).
- Hit ball from a 'tee' (e.g. ball set on post for rounders, rather than bowled).
- Use adapted equipment (e.g. large bats, balls).

Scoring:

Disabled players may:

- Use lower nets (i.e. tennis, basketball, netball).
- Use hoop placed on floor (i.e. basketball, netball).
- Use larger scoring areas (i.e. tennis).
- Use different boundaries (i.e. cricket, rounders).

Useful Addresses

ACE Access Centre, 1 Broadbent Road, Oldham OL1 4HV.

ACE Centre, Ormerod School, Waynflete Road, Headington, Oxford OX3 8DO.

CENMAC *(Information Technology)*, Charlton Park School, Charlton Park Road, London SE7 8HX.

Centre for Studies of Inclusive Education (CSIE), 1 Redland Close, Elm Lane, Redland, Bristol BS6 6UE.

Concept Keyboard Co. *(Information Technology)*, Moarside Road, Winnal Industrial Estate, Winchester, Hampshire SO23 7RX.

Contact a Family, 170 Tottenham Court Road, London W1P 0HA.

Disabled Sports *(England)*, Maryglen Haigh Suite, Solecast House, 13–27 Brunswick Place, London N1 6DX.

Foundation for Communication for the Disabled, Foundation House, 25 High Street, Woking, Surrey GU21 1BW.

National Council for Educational Technology, Millburn Hill Road, Science Park, Coventry CV4 7JJ.

Nottingham Rehab *(Specialist and adapted equipment)*, Ludlow Hill Road, West Bridgford, Nottingham NG2 6HD.

Royal National Institute for the Blind, National Education Services, Garrow House, 190 Kensal Road, London W10 5BT.

Simnett Computers *(Special needs hardware and software)*, Fifth floor, Alperton House, Bridgewater Road, Wembley, Middlesex.

Vari-Tech *(Manufacturers of education furniture)*, Atkinson Engineering, Unit 4, Sett End Road, Blackburn, Lancashire BB1 2PT.

Wheelchair Corporation Ltd. *(Stairclimbing and standing up solutions)*, Incmoor House, Chelmarsh, Bridgnorth, Shropshire WV16 6AZ.

References

Bangs, J. (1995) 'Facilities for pupils with SEN including facilities which increase or assist access to the school by pupils who are disabled, in *SEN policy pack*. Council for Disabled Children.

Coopers & Lybrand (1992) 'Within Reach: Access for Disabled Children - Mainstream Education'. NUT/The Spastics Society.

Cowne E. (1996) *The SENCO Handbook. Working within a whole school approach.* David Fulton.

DFEE (1994) *Code of Practice on the Identification and Assessment of Special Educational Needs*. Department for Education.

Hill, W. (1996) 'Spotlight on Special Educational Needs – Physical Disabilities', in *Spotlight on Educational Needs*, Kenward, H. NASEN.

Mason, M. (1995) 'The Inclusive Classroom' – Discussion Paper III. *Schools' Special Needs Policies Pack*. National Children's Bureau.

McCarthy, D. and Davies, J. (1996) *The SEN Resource Manual for Schools – Specialist Matters*.

Mitler, P. (1995) 'Special Needs Education: an international perspective'. *British Journal of Special Education* **22**(3).

Norwich, B. (1995) Discussion Paper II. *Schools' Special Needs Policy Pack*. National Children's Bureau.

Oliver, M. (1988) 'The Social and political context of education policy: The case of special needs, in *The Policies of Special Educational Needs*, L. Barton (ed.). Falmer Press.

Ratiamim, L. (1993) 'Access to Words and Images – Using information technology to support the learning of students with physical disabilities'. NCET/CENMAC.

Reiser, R. (1995) 'Developing a whole-school approach to inclusion: making the most of the Code and the 1993 Act: a personal view' – Discussion Paper III. *Schools' Special Needs Policies Pack*. National Children's Bureau.

TVEI SE Race and Gender Network (1988) 'Managing the Process of Promoting Equality of Opportunity'. Training, Enterprise & Education Directorate.

United Nations. *The Convention of the Rights of the Child*. Adapted by the General Assembly on 20 November 1989 and entered into force on 2 September 1990. New York: UN 1989.

UNESCO. The Salamanca World Conference Declaration. Paris. UNESCO 1994.

Ward, B. (1993) *Healing Grief – A guide to loss and recovery*. London: Vermilion.

Ward B. and associates (1995) *Good Grief – Exploring feelings of loss and death with under elevens*. London: Jessica Kingsley Publications.